Fatal Call of the Running Tide

Also by Barry Cockcroft

Hannah In Yorkshire
The Ways Of a Yorkshire Dale
The Dale That Died
Princes Of The Plough
Ball Of Fire
Romany Summer
Seasons Of My Life
Daughter Of The Dales
Hannah: The Complete Story
A Celebration Of Yorkshire
Innocent Abroad
Hannah's North Country
Hannah In America

FATAL CALL OF THE RUNNING TIDE

Lifeboat Rescues and Sea Dramas

Barry Cockcroft

Hodder & Stoughton

First published in 1995
by Hodder and Stoughton
A division of Hodder Headline PLC

10 9 8 7 6 5 4 3 2 1

British Library Cataloguing in Publication Data
Cockcroft, Barry
Fatal Call of the Running Tide
I. Title
823 [F]

ISBN 0 340 63524 X

Typeset by Palimpsest Book Production Limited,
Polmont, Stirlingshire
Printed and bound in Great Britain by
Mackays of Chatham PLC, Chatham, Kent

Hodder and Stoughton
A division of Hodder Headline PLC
338 Euston Road
London NW1 3BH

For Sarah and Lucy, my gale-force girls,
and Celia, my rescuer.

Acknowledgements

Barry Cockcroft extends much gratitude to all the admirable people who feature in this book. Without their co-operation and trust, it would not have been possible.

Particular thanks are due to Edward Wake-Walker, the RNLI's Head of Public Relations, for guiding the research unerringly in the right direction.

Also to the administrative staff at the RNLI's headquarters in Poole, Dorset; to numerous honorary secretaries throughout the United Kingdom and Ireland; to Vivien Green, Roland Philipps, Angela Herlihy and Rosemary Volante.

Contents

List of Illustrations

Colour Section

Prologue

'A Wild Call and a Clear Call . . .'

A certain species of people lives in bittersweet conflict with one of the supreme forces of nature. Traditionally merciless, occasionally generous, it rules their days and their nights and fashions their existence – even the way they look – in such a manner that they are distanced physically and spiritually from ordinary mortals.

At the cutting edge of this species are the men who must answer the call of the running tide, who choose to live by what the sea will give them.

Too often it is a fatal call, as a long and ever-growing roll call of widows and fatherless children around the rim of these islands eloquently and bleakly testifies.

This book is about the way of life in a small cross section of 210 communities clinging to the shores of Great Britain and Ireland, poised each dawn for the chance to scoop a netful of fish to pay the rent, to bring their cargo safely to port or to snatch a life from the fury of a storm.

Each of these particular communities is distinguished by a building defiantly perched as close to the sea as discretion allows, flying a flag with the Cross of St George on a white background. The centre is emblazoned with a crown and anchor, and each quarter bears a letter – R. N. L. I.

The Royal National Lifeboat Institution can claim to be truly unique – bearing no allegiance to vested interests or government bodies, financially dependent on nothing but the generosity of the public, beholden to no authority save its own.

It exists solely to fight a war it knows it can never win, and has waged it for more than 170 years. Its frontline troops are all volunteers. Nations fight wars, one against the other. Man against man, machine against machine. Eventually there is a resolution, if only temporary. But there can never be peace, not for a moment, for the men who serve under the flag bearing that particular cross of the dragon-slayer. Their enemy is the most enigmatic of all.

To most of them it is also the provider of life. They ask it every day for the means to pay the mortgage, to feed and clothe their children.

Just to be a fisherman in these islands is dangerous enough, for the seas in which they are planted are among the most treacherous in the world. To also be a lifeboatman is to multiply the risk tenfold at least. There are few, if any, who cannot tell a tale of the time they thought their lives were about to end. Many didn't survive to tell it.

And yet . . . to be a senior member of a lifeboat crew, to be granted a regular jacket, is one of the most signal honours these communities can bestow. They certainly don't do it for material rewards. And to become coxswain commands a respect which cannot be measured.

Most of you will have met, or at least seen lifeboatmen since they invariably inhabit many of the pretty places where the nation goes to play. You may have bought their fresh fish, gone with them on trips round the the bay in their working boats – they must take their living wherever they can find it – without realising the extra responsibility they bear. Apart from their nautical attire, and features usually rough-hewn by the constant assault of the elements, they do not appear to be particularly special.

But they are.

Venture now on a privileged odyssey, a journey around two islands visiting outposts of this rare breed, which for generations has answered the curious, often deadly call of the running tide.

Barry Cockcroft

1

Survivor

I have seen old ships sail like swans asleep . . .
With leaden age o'ercargoed

Amid the swirling holiday crowds in St Ives, Cornwall, could often be seen the figure of an elderly man, leaning against the quayside rails. Below him children laughed and dug in the sand and splashed out in the shallows to peer into the flotilla of small fishing boats at anchor in the harbour.

A cacophony of sound and visual distractions were all around him, but the old man seemed totally unaware. He would gaze silently out to sea, as still as if carved from the same weathered granite as the buildings circling the wharf. His features spoke of past suffering, like an old pugilist.

Occasionally, a passing local fisherman would greet him in a most curious way:

''Morning, Survivor.'

It would earn him a nod, for speech did not come easily to this man. Nor did movement, for he walked with a studied, deliberate gait. And yet . . . some would say he was the most fortunate man in St Ives. Others might say the least.

For William Freeman, during one terrible January night more than half a century ago, lost everything – except his life. His way of life, his confidence, his health, even his name.

William Freeman lived for and from the sea, like his forebears. A fisherman since childhood, he was one of the eighty men who, in the old days, would launch the St Ives lifeboat by sheer muscle power. Forty men to a rope, up to the neck in freezing seawater.

William, then aged thirty-six, was there when the maroons went up in the small hours of 23 January 1939, as the worst storm in the memory of anyone alive lashed the sea outside the harbour with awesome fury. Coastguards had reported a ship in distress off the Cornish coast.

When Tommy Cocking, known to everyone as Bar, the sixty-five-year-old coxswain, positioned his new, self-righting motor lifeboat at the top of the slipway and looked around him he saw he had only five crewmen. Other regular members of his team had not heard the maroons, so fierce was the din of the elements. He needed eight.

Bellowing against the roar of a ninety-mile-an-hour hurricane, as the town's womenfolk looked fearfully on, he called men by name.

'Take a jacket, will ye?' he said three times.

And three times a man stepped out of the milling crowd, accepted the cork and canvas jacket held out to him and climbed aboard.

Suddenly there was another delay. One of the three men who had accepted a jacket turned to Tommy Cocking and said: 'Give it to someone else, Bar,' and climbed out of the lifeboat, handing back the jacket as he did so.

To realise the significance of this action, it is necessary to understand something of the complex nature of the St Ives seagoing community, which is knitted tightly together by much intermarriage . . . and danger.

The stunned silence which greeted this momentous declaration – even the banshee howl of the hurricane seemed to diminish momentarily – was broken by William Freeman.

'Will I do, Bar?' he said.

Tommy Cocking looked gratefully at Freeman. 'You'll do, William,' he said. 'Take a jacket.'

William Freeman shrugged aside his frantic wife and climbed aboard. Her cries of despair swelled the chorus of the other womenfolk watching their men being dragged by ropes into the boiling surf.

As it left the safety of the harbour, the *John and Sarah Eliza Stych*, a modern thirty-five-footer, was dwarfed by mountainous seas, but struggled on in the direction of Cape Cornwall. Eleven sea miles away, across one of the deadliest stretches of seaway in Europe, a ship had been spotted in terminal trouble. It was never seen again and was presumed sunk with all hands.

The St Ives lifeboat covered scarcely one-tenth of the way. If it had not been night, the people of St Ives would have been able to watch their lifeboat and their men tumble over and over, crushed and hammered across St Ives bay.

The story of what happened comes hesitantly, in a choked voice from Survivor. The sole survivor. Amazingly, William Freeman stepped ashore straight from the boat after it had been hurled on to a cliff ledge like a child's toy.

William Freeman and his wife, Margaret, would not have been able to sleep that night apart from the storm because one of their two young daughters had been ill for weeks. Her sleep was disturbed and they were worried that the torrential rain would come through the roof on to her bed because violent gusts were ripping slates off the roof of their house close to the harbour. So they were both up in the small hours moving the children's beds into the middle of the bedroom.

'Then I looked out of the window and saw that all the lights were on in the lifeboat house, so I thought they must be getting ready for something,' said William.

'I was just in the middle of undressing for bed when the maroons went off. So I got my clothes back on and went down to the slipway. When I got there the lifeboat was stopped on the top of the slip. Someone had given his jacket back to the box. He asked for another volunteer.

'I said I would go. I couldn't tell you why. I had never served in that boat before, only been in the old sailing lifeboat. I just said I'd go at once. So I buckled the jacket on whilst another crewman tried to comfort my wife. Her brother was on the boat, too, you see. She was told to go home, that the boat was as safe as houses.'

It was a low-water launch and as the crew struggled to make the rudder operational, the boat headed out of control towards rocks. Just in time, they managed to veer away and vanished into the night.

'It didn't seem as if we had gone very far when a big sea hit the starboard bow and she capsized. Four men went out that time, including the cox and the wife's brother. I heard one call out but never saw any of them again.

'When the boat righted itself, I found myself hanging over the side with some rope. Someone gave me a hand aboard. The anchor was dropped but it wasn't long before it snapped like a carrot. The engine had stopped automatically like it was supposed to during a capsize and the engineer was trying to start her up again when she capsized again. And he was gone.

'I had managed to get under the canopy with two other men and I shouted out to them: "Hang on, boys, it'll take us ashore somewhere!" Then it capsized a third time, and I saw the other two go. So I was by myself . . . but I didn't have much time to think before she started to capsize again – and landed on her side on the rocks on the far side of the bay. I just stepped ashore.

'Many's the time I've thought to myself: How didn't those two hang on for just another minute?'

The sole survivor still had to fight for his life as he scrambled up the cliff face with waves breaking over him, trying to pull him back to join his seven drowned seamates. He abandoned his waterlogged boots and managed to find a farmhouse, where they took care of him, putting him to bed surrounded by hot-water bottles. When he finally arrived home late in the afternoon, his wife scarcely recognised him. He had received a terrible beating from the sea, and his face was grotesquely swollen.

It took some hours before the news of the disaster reached St Ives, since the storm had blown down telephone lines. And when it did, no one wanted to be the one to break the news to the families of those on the *John and Sarah Eliza Stych*. Margaret Freeman was up at dawn seeking news when she encountered a neighbour in the street.

'She said: "Isn't it just awful, Margaret?" And I said that yes, the weather was dreadful. And then she said: "No – I mean the lifeboat."

'The lifeboat! What do you mean, the lifeboat? My husband and my brother are on that boat.

'Well, she looked horrified. Next thing she had vanished, flew like the wind. Of course, I started crying and went to see my mother – and she knew nothing about it, either.'

When the dire reality finally dawned, the entire community went into deep mourning. Every other cottage curtain was drawn as a mark of respect, for nearly everyone in the fishing families of St Ives was a cousin of some kind to everyone else.

William Freeman never went on board a boat again. Even a walk along the pier presented problems.

'One day I was watching a boat going out and she started rolling a bit. I had to turn away. I felt sick.'

He died on 23 January 1979 – forty years to the hour after the launch that ruined his life.

There is another side to this tragic event: the story of the man who gave back the jacket. He is dead now, too, and he was an old man before he decided to tell it publicly. Even the children of those directly involved in the affairs of that dramatic night had been unaware of the part John Stevens played.

'I went down that night thinking I'd give them a hand to launch. I wasn't a member of the crew. Anyway, they were short, I was asked to go and I agreed. So I climbed aboard and picked up this jacket. It felt like a lump of lead in my hands, and they're only featherweight really. I was starting to go over the side to put it on when I heard voices . . . voices. So I looked and looked, but there was nobody there. But the voices came louder and louder, buzzing in my two ears. Plain speech. "Drop that jacket! . . . Drop that jacket!"

'It was incessant. And it stopped me. I thought – Yes, I've heard them before. My angels. So I went to the coxswain and asked him to give the jacket to someone else.'

That decision was to affect the remainder of John Stevens' life, too. Not one member of the fishing community of St Ives, among whom he spent a lifetime as a successful boat owner, ever mentioned the incident – to him. Close to four decades of silence on the subject which clearly echoed within him as incessantly as those voices.

'No – not one, from that day to this,' he said with the infinite sadness of someone who dearly wished the ghost of that night could have been exorcised by the counselling of his closest colleagues.

'And William Freeman and I have not spoken one word to each other since then, although he's married to a first cousin of mine. We pass each other in the streets most days. The rest of my family speak to him. But not me.'

After a time he stopped going to the cosy wooden lodges with brightly burning coal fires built on the quayside so that old fishermen could meet, brew a pot of tea and exchange familiar yarns about the exploits of days gone by.

But in their declining years, their respective wives gently conspired with a television programme, and a meeting between William Freeman and John Stevens was finally brought about.

It was an emotional moment for both of them. A heavy burden lifted at last.

2

Capsize!

Capsize is the word which freezes the blood of any seaman. It always means total disorientation, complete loss of control and, almost inevitably, loss of life. By the very nature of their calling, lifeboatmen habitually place themselves at extreme risk of their vessel's capsize, which is why all the big boats are self-righting. When a lifeboat is rolled over the engines stop automatically, and within five or six seconds it will have corrected its position with no action required from the crew.

Just as well, since the crew will have spent those seconds – very long seconds in the circumstances – trying to hang on underwater, using any bit of the boat near to hand, and may be injured or swept away at worst, or completely bemused at best. Then attempting to regain control with men and equipment lying in untidy heaps around the boat, and the sea probably doing its utmost to repeat the trauma.

Most – possibly all – lifeboat disasters such as the one which shattered the St Ives community started with a capsize. In the entire history of the RNLI it is said that only two capsizes have ended without fatal consequences. The last was on 28 February 1993 and the circumstances almost defy belief. One man, certainly, was incredibly fortunate to survive.

The Hartlepool lifeboat has an illustrious history stretching back almost 200 years. It was founded in 1803. Most RNLI stations are positioned in places of undoubted visual appeal, but not the Hartlepool boat. It is stationed amid the inevitable squalor of a northeastern dockyard which appears to have known more prosperous times.

Young, fit men form the nucleus of the Hartlepool crew, and most come from nautical backgrounds although diminishing opportunities in seafaring occupations have forced some to seek employment ashore. Paul Watson, the second coxswain, is one example. His background is a classic example of a shoreline family engaged in a variety of activities trying to earn a living from the sea. His father always had a boat, potting for crabs and lobsters, taking out fishing parties in the season, doing jobs around the docks – and seacoling.

Seacoaling is peculiar to a part of the northeast coast where the pits work seams of coal. Some seams continue in shallow lines under the seabed and a strenuous ground sea can churn up the coal, wash it and deposit it along the tide line.

'My dad had an old army wagon to load it on,' said Paul, who was born in 1960. 'It was hard, cold and messy work, but he made a bit of a living at it, selling to households and even coal merchants. I helped him as a kid, and it was good enough at one time for Dad to hire one or two men.

'I went fishing when I left school because the sea was in my blood, made a little bit with my first boats and bought a forty-foot trawler. But the fish stocks went down, so did the prices and I started making a loss. I was forced to sell the trawler and go to work in a chicken factory, but I still managed to run a little boat.'

Ian Gilbraith, the lifeboat mechanic, born five years earlier than Paul, hails from a similar background. Son of a marine engineer, he ran fishing trips and set up a business with a partner repairing and selling boats. He tells a story of one trip which had fourteen people contentedly fishing for codling and whiting on a lovely calm day three miles out to sea. Ian happened to notice that the boat's exhaust pipe was a little low in the water so he decided to check the engine room. It was a good metre underwater – the pipe had come off the bilge pump and it was siphoning the sea back into the boat.

'I had to avoid panic among the clients, so I quietly told my partner and stood him by to help. I took my shirt and trousers off, and went under the water to try and find the pipe to repair it. Somehow I managed, told my mate to switch on the pump and thankfully it worked. Then I got myself dried off and dressed and then I walked casually among the party, helping out and generally giving advice. They had no idea we were so close – less than half an hour – from sinking. If I hadn't noticed that exhaust it would have been a Mayday call for the lifeboat.'

Ian became interested in joining the lifeboat when he was on another fishing trip. The weather turned 'shabby' – the northeastern word for it – and Ian made all speed for the shelter of the harbour.

'Everyone was running for cover that day, including the professional fishing boats. We were one of the last to make it and by then it had really turned nasty – time to offer up a little prayer. Then just as we were coming into the harbour the lifeboat was going out.

'I thought – Christ! There's still somebody out there and they need help. I was so grateful that there was someone prepared to put out in those conditions to save people in distress that I volunteered to serve. That was thirteen years ago, and now I am the full-time mechanic.'

Ian (but not Paul) was on the lifeboat on that momentous February day in 1993. It had started innocently with a launching exercise in the morning with some local dignitaries on board. Among the crew was the man who against all the odds cheated what under normal circumstances would have been certain death. They speak of him at the RNLI Headquarters in Poole, Dorset, in awed tones.

He is Robert Maiden, twenty-seven-year-old son of a father who served as coxswain on the Hartlepool boat for fourteen years and won the bronze medal. For generations the Maiden family have run the foyboats in the harbour, picking up lines from large boats seeking to dock and helping them to tie up. Robert has a brother, Ian, four years younger, who also serves on the lifeboat.

That day the lifeboat went through its paces for the benefit of the dignitaries, but a gale began to blow and a blizzard added to the misery so they were all glad to return. The weather expectations that day had not been good but the forecast fell far short of reality. And Hartlepool Bay is traditionally subject to the menace of broken water.

'We got back and fuelled up and I thought: Smashing – we'll go for a couple of pints,' recalled Ian Gilbraith.

'We were just on our second pint and looking forward to going home for a meal when the pagers went off. First, the harbour master said the Teesmouth lifeboat was in trouble, and then announced that a tanker had gone aground on Redcar beach about four miles away, which confused us a bit. So we launched with the cox, Eric Reeve, at the helm. When we arrived on the scene we saw the Teesmouth boat laid off about a mile away. It had suffered what we call an "updown", a wave hitting the stern and turning the boat virtually 360 degrees around to the starboard, reversing one of the engines and knocking oil seals out of one of the fuel pumps. So they had only one engine working, and since a force eight to nine northeasterly was blowing they limped back to station leaving us to it. But there was nothing really that we could do.

'The rescue helicopter had lifted some of the crew off the tanker until the skipper ordered them to stop. She was a big ship, high and dry on the beach, and in no danger and he needed men to crew it.

'We were just standing off the tanker waiting for instructions, heading north at about six knots and feeling miserable, wondering what we were doing out there. It was pitch-black, the snow was pelting down and we were soaking wet and cold. We did hit a mass of broken water which shook us around a bit but we got safely through it into a calm patch and the boredom began again. Then it happened.

'This massive, great breaking wave came out of nowhere and lifted us straight up into the air. The boat literally fell over backwards – it did a back flip. That wave was about as high as the boat was long – forty-five feet. We were upside down, all hanging on and swirling about until it righted itself – that took about five or six seconds. Then another wave came and tipped us over again. The engines were down, the mast was down and a two-hundredweight towing reel had broken off and was rolling around the deck when we came up again, which could have smashed the legs of the crew. But the lads managed to haul it into a well and lash it down.

'I flicked the capsize switches on the console to engage the engines again, and managed to get down below to inspect the engine room where I found a foot and a half of water. One of the lads below had done a couple of somersaults and hurt his neck. You could see the blood from his injuries on the ceiling. So I told him to stay put. Eric Reeve was hanging on to the wheel all the time watching out for the next wave. I did a crew count. One man was missing.'

It was Robert Maiden.

The missing man takes up the story: 'I saw the wave coming. At the time I was sitting on the life raft just behind the wheelhouse. I heard Tommy Price shouting, "Just look at the size of this bugger," so I unclipped my lifeline and tried to get into the wheelhouse. But it was crammed in there – no room for me. If I had stayed where I was when the wave hit it would have broken my back, because I was pressed against a steel scaffolding bar and there were sixty tons of water coming at me.

'So I hung on to the wire mesh behind the cox's seat, but the boat came up at such an angle that I fell back on to the life raft where I managed to wrap my arms around a handrail. Then it was all white water and I felt my legs lifting over the top of my head. That must have been when the boat fell backwards over the top of the wave. There was a big tug, and I was gone.'

On the boat, Ian Gilbraith was trying to call for help. 'But all the electrics had blown – sparks and shocks all over the place. I tried to put out a Mayday on the medium-frequency set, but it was loose and rattly inside. I think someone in Germany heard us, that's all! So I passed the hand-held radio to Ian, Robert's brother, and asked him to call a Mayday.'

The brother of the missing man was in a sorry state himself. He weighs twenty stones and the capsize had flung him across the wheelhouse, up against the deck head and straight into the cox's seat, knocking him down and taking the seat straight off its mounts, shearing the half-inch stainless-steel bolts. He landed on top of Ian Gilbraith.

'At that point the boat rolled completely upside down,' said Ian. 'I grabbed the wire mesh grid at the back of the wheelhouse and hung there next to the cox, suspended under water. The second time the boat went over I lost my grip and was washed on to the deck where I managed to reach what was left of the towing reel and hung on again. Everybody except Gary Jameson, who was at the back of the wheelhouse, had unclipped their lifelines to change positions so it was lucky we weren't all swept overboard. I was swirled around like a rag doll but I was determined not to let go this time, and as a result I stretched every muscle in my left arm, pulled all the joints out about half an inch and consequently every time I pull a rope now, particularly when it's cold, those joints start to ache.

'I ended up with my legs dangling over the side. Then another wave struck and we went up through ninety degrees but that time we didn't capsize.'

Ian Maiden quickly overcame the pain and confusion and sent out the Mayday, which mercifully was heard by the rescue helicopter which had finished its business with the tanker and was just taking off from Redcar beach after refuelling. Then he learned that his brother was no longer on board.

A frantic search began. Their hopes were raised when they twice thought they had spotted the light from Robert's life jacket, but once it was the man overboard buoy, which lights up when filled with water, and next it was the life raft which had automatically inflated in the water. Both had been swept from the boat. The crew did their best to comb the area but had to contend with more giant waves which did more damage to the boat.

Meanwhile, the man they were looking for was trying to cope with his desperate situation, alone at night in a furious sea with snow and sleet slanting down.

'After the capsize, I was under water for what seemed quite a while – maybe fifteen or twenty seconds. Then I popped up and saw the lifeboat about fifty yards away. I was very concerned because I couldn't see anyone on board and I wondered whether there was anyone else in the water with me. I shouted, and looked around, then another wave came and I was bowled around in the surf. When I came up again the boat was around 100 yards away, and still I couldn't see anyone.

'Then I had to think what to do. It was at the back of my mind that I might not survive, that not many people had been where I was and made it back, but I knew that there would be a good bunch of lads looking for me.

'Just before the capsize we had broken into the packs of sweets that we keep on board, and I had put some fruit pastilles in one of my pockets. After I had been in the water for about fifteen minutes I thought I would have a fruit pastille and reached for the packet. They had been bloody well washed out!

'The waves were still rolling me around, but I had blown up my life jacket as hard as I could to get the most buoyancy, and pulled my coat over my head to prevent getting a mouthful of salt water with every wave. I had set my detachable light off on my life jacket and was waving it around as much as I could. I also tightened the straps on my oilskins to retain the water, so it would warm up like a wet suit. After I had been in the water about twenty minutes I saw a Nimrod aircraft go over, which lifted my spirits for a while because it meant they were trying to find me. But then I began to get colder and colder, until I lost all feeling in my arms. I kept checking the time on my watch and after another ten minutes I saw a helicopter doing a search pattern. Then it began to hover about 200 or 300 yards away from me. Apparently it had spotted the life raft. I started shouting and splashing with my arms and legs hoping that my light would catch the spray I was kicking up, but it was still snowing and pitch-black.

'Then by sheer chance, the copilot happened to glance in my direction and spotted me. They winched me out and got me to hospital. When they measured my body temperature they told me I had been fifteen minutes away from certain death.

'I also found out that the rest of the crew were all right, which was a great relief because I thought something terrible had happened to them. They had already got the news on the radio that I had been found. Then came a great moment for me. I was sitting in a cubicle wrapped up in tinfoil like a Christmas turkey when the nurses whipped back the curtains and I saw the rest of the crew coming into Casualty.

'They were on stretchers, they were limping, heads bandaged, but it was a great reunion and we all had a good laugh.

'Looking back, I realise just how amazingly fortunate I was. In ordinary clothes a man will last about ten to fifteen minutes in a winter sea. By sheer chance I was also wearing thermal underwear as well as my oilskins, which I don't do normally. And what are the chances of a helicopter being on the spot and fully operational two or three miles away from a capsize, not to mention being spotted by pure accident?

'Someone was looking after me that day.'

After such an experience it would have been only reasonable if, like poor William Freeman in St Ives, Robert Maiden had quit the lifeboat, maybe declined to go aboard a boat ever again. But together with the rest of the crew, he has decided that nothing worse can possibly happen to them in the lifeboat, and if he can survive what he did then, he can survive anything.

And he proceeded to prove not only that he meant it, but that he possesses courage of a special kind. Less than a week after that terrible ordeal, he was aboard the inflatable inshore lifeboat racing to the rescue of a man washed up on the rocks along the coast.

3

Man Overboard!

There can be no more devastating moment for a lifeboat crew battling to save other lives than when they realise that one of their own has been swept overboard . . . in the sure knowledge that his chances of survival are far from certain. Much less so at night. But one man in the spring of 1994 was placed in a nightmare position, when the situation clearly demanded that he must leave, even if briefly, his close colleague and friend to the mercy of the sea.

Although he had been a crew member for over twenty-four years, Mike Bowden had only been the cox of the Appledore lifeboat in North Devon for less than three months. This particular mission had seemed at first to present no special difficulties – the lifeboat had been called to assist in towing a broken-down motor yacht with three men aboard.

But there is one permanent hazard for anyone sailing in or out of Appledore – the Bideford Bar, recognised as one of the worst of its kind in the world. It has claimed many lives down the years. Joe Ball, Chairman of the Appledore RNLI and an experienced seaman himself, described it as a terrible place.

'Even when the weather is reasonably mild, there can be confused seas in the narrow channel leading from the open sea into the estuary, and when there are thirty-foot spring tides rushing in between the sandbanks it is an awesome sight. And if a southwesterly blows up, then any boat is in trouble.'

Mike Bowden and his crew reached the motor yacht around

Hartland Point without incident, and took it under tow. But there was a force six blowing, ominously from the southwest.

'The men on the yacht were a bit out of it so I put one of our crew members, Mike Weekes, aboard to organise things. Everything was coming along quite fine at first but then the wind suddenly freshened. Still, the entrance to the bar seemed quite good, so we started to steam towards it. Then some big seas started rolling in so I decided to turn and go back out to await a bit more flood tide when the waves would subside. But the boat under tow hit a couple of nasty seas on the turn and was swamped. Mike had put the three crew in the cabin and was unfortunately still outside himself when a guardrail gave way and he was washed overboard.

'We pulled the yacht to the stern of our boat, got the three men into our after cabin and cut the casualty adrift so we could go and look for Mike. We radioed for the inshore boat, which can search in shallow water close to the bar, and alerted the helicopter.

'By that time it was dark, so we fired parachute flares and used both our searchlights but we still couldn't spot him. Neither could the inshore boat. Although we knew he was well kitted up in a new life jacket issued by the RNLI, we also knew he couldn't last long in water that cold. It didn't bear thinking about.'

The moment arrived which will doubtless haunt Mike Bowden for the rest of his life. It was the first major incident for the Appledore boat during his command and he had to face up to a decision which no man would relish.

'As we were searching, one of the crew came up to me and told me that the three men below in the cabin were suffering from hypothermia and shock, and their condition was deteriorating. They needed urgent hospital treatment. After conferring with other crew members, I decided we must leave the scene and get them ashore. I called for our boarding boat to come and meet us, and steamed away over the bar.

'Having transferred the men successfully, we were heading back as fast as we could to resume searching for Mike when the news came on the radio. The helicopter had spotted him in its night sights, had picked him out and he was OK.

'I cannot even begin to tell you how relieved I was to hear that news. And the rest of the crew, too, of course.'

Mike Weekes had been in the water for forty-five minutes, and his core temperature was dangerously low. He had been swept a quarter of a mile away from the bar to the surf near Saunton Sands. Apparently, he wouldn't have survived more than another ten or fifteen minutes. He was put into intensive care for twenty-four hours.

When the two met up again afterwards it was an emotional moment.

'You're a bloody sight for sore eyes,' was the coxswain's first comment.

Fortunately Mike happens to be one of the fittest men in the crew, in his mid-thirties and strong. He works as both a crane driver at a local shipyard and as a local fisherman in his spare time. And he is still a leading member of the Appledore lifeboat crew despite that experience. Indeed, he insisted on going out again at the earliest possible opportunity.

It seems that Appledore men are traditionally hard and physically powerful, brought up as they are to seafaring and building ships, as chairman Joe Ball can confirm. He first came to Appledore in 1952 from the Sunderland area to help run the shipyard, when 900 men were employed there. He eventually became managing director. The recession has halved that workforce in recent years.

'When I arrived I realised that to win the respect of men like this I would have to show them I could do the same job as them. So I put on overalls for the first time in years and I got to work swinging a hammer and an adze. That way I built up team spirit and became accepted as someone who knew the job thoroughly, not just another man in a suit. Appledore village has a population of only around 3,000 and there are one or two families who have been there for generations, noted for being tough and willing workers. We had one man working in the dockyard who, although not very tall, was the strongest man around. Jack Eastman was his name, nicknamed Daddy.

'I used to do weightlifting at the time and I thought I was pretty good. One day a man was picking up fifty-six-pound weights and I wanted to show everybody that the boss could do it, too. I lifted a couple of them, one gripped in each hand. Whereupon old Jack Eastman laughed and promptly picked them up just using a finger and thumb!'

One of the oldest established Appledore families is named Cox, aptly since so many of them served on the lifeboat. In 1993 there was a 'Cox Day' to honour two of them, Joe Cox, coxswain from

1852 to 1873, and his son, Joe Junior, cox from 1873 to 1891. The family presented some of their medals to the North Devon Maritime Museum.

Another Cox, apparently unrelated, became a very distinguished coxswain himself between 1970 and 1994, when he retired after thirty-six years of service. Desmond Cox, son of a second cox, and the grandson of William Cox, who came from Ireland to settle in Appledore when he married a local girl, had a curious story to tell about his grandfather.

'He was eighteen at the time and was on watch one night on a square-rigger. His shipmates came to relieve him in the morning and he had been struck deaf and dumb. Nobody ever found out why, apparently not even my grandmother. He could write, but never attempted to explain in that way. I remember being carried about on his shoulders as a child and he communicated with me by hand signals. After it happened he gave up sailing around the world and worked as a fisherman, and also served on the lifeboat.

'I first went to sea myself under sail at the age of fifteen in 1954, one of the last Appledore lads to do so, doing coastal work in a two-masted ketch to begin with and eventually moving to steam vessels trading in the Bristol Channel. I became a chief officer at the age of seventeen and captain at twenty.'

Desmond joined the Appledore crew in 1958, and in 1966 was involved in a drama which was extraordinary, even by lifeboat standards. It started on the evening of New Year's Day when a message was received from Lundy Isle that a woman had suffered a miscarriage, was haemorrhaging badly and needed urgent medical assistance. And plasma. The weather was so atrocious that the helicopter from RAF Chivenor could not get off the ground.

'It was a norwest force ten. We had to wait until after low water to stand any chance of getting across Bideford Bar. Two doctors came with us and it took us five hours to do what was normally a two-hour trip. We received such a pounding over the bar that the bowman, who was sitting on the deck in the cabin, holding on tight to a flask of blood plasma, was thrown four feet in the air against the roof and knocked unconscious. So he was the first casualty treated by the doctors that night.

'We reached Lundy at midnight, and they launched two beach boats to take the doctors ashore. But they both capsized, and finished up on the rocks. There were no casualties, fortunately.

At half-past one in the morning we were all getting disillusioned when someone came up with an idea. There was a wire running about 600 feet from the cliffs on the southeast tip of Lundy to an anchor in the middle of the bay. It was used to send supplies on a pulley up to the lighthouse. It had a barrel kind of breeches buoy, so the cox, "Bosun" Carter, carefully manoeuvred the boat so that the stern was up to the wire and signalled for the barrel to be sent down. The doctors were winched up by hand, one at a time, in the teeth of a hurricane. I wouldn't have gone up in that thing myself, but I think those two were glad to get off the lifeboat.'

Dr William Ruddock, and Dr Gordon Brook, survived the trip – and saved the woman's life. She was taken off to hospital by helicopter the following day. And the names of the doctors are inscribed in the Book of Valour at the British Medical Association headquarters.

The lifeboat itself couldn't get back over the bar to Appledore that day and was forced to return to Lundy for shelter. She finally reached home after forty hours at sea. Apparently, if they had failed to deliver the doctors at the time they did, the woman would have died.

No medals were awarded by the RNLI.

Proceeding from the sublime to the ridiculous, there is another episode in the colourful history of the Appledore lifeboat which is, by total contrast, completely rooted in farce. It was the time they arrested a drunk driver.

The man in question had been chased through Bideford by the police. He drove along the quay and went straight down the slipway into the river, completely submerging his car. Two young men happened to be testing diving gear nearby at the time and together they pulled him out of the car. They were helping him up the slipway when he spotted the police waiting for him, broke free and jumped back into the water. He swam out to a powerboat and climbed in. To everyone's amazement it burst into life. It turned out that it was his boat, and he had the ignition keys on him. He roared off towards the old bridge in Bideford, which has twenty-six arches, all different sizes. The police called the lifeboat station, which seemed to be the only option. The inshore boat was launched, came to the slipway, and took two policemen on board. Then they gave chase.

According to a witness, the affair then became even more bizarre – 'like a cross between a Keystone Cops comedy and a James Bond movie, with the two boats racing up and down the river for five or ten minutes, and flying through the arches time after time.'

The RNLI boat had the edge in speed, and eventually managed to lock on to the powerboat. One of the crew leaped across and switched off the engine, followed by the two policemen who effected an arrest.

The man, duly dealt with in the courts, was not added to the list of lives saved on the Roll of Honour in the Appledore lifeboat house, which had exceeded 740 in 1994.

Neither was the horse. The animal in question threw its female rider on the beach at Appledore and, for reasons best known to itself, headed out to sea. This turned into a comedy drama, with the lifeboat, the rescue helicopter and the fire brigade in attendance.

The lifeboat caught up with the horse, a keen swimmer, just before it reached the open sea where the riptide would have swept it away at a rate of knots. The crew solicitously managed to attach a long rope to it so that it wouldn't have to be close to the engines and gently pulled it ashore. However, when the horse found its feet on the beach again there was another crisis. The helicopter, and all the people running around, caused it to bolt again. It ran into some rocks and became wedged.

The fire brigade was summoned. One very full hour after the alarm was first raised, a team of lifeboat- and firemen gingerly reversed the horse out of the rocks and led it down to the beach.

Whereupon the lady remounted, and gratefully rode off into the sunset.

4

'Those Infernal Ribble Banks' – and the Lighter Side of Lifeboat Service

Humour and drama are often closely partnered in the human condition. Curiously, the lifeboat station which was hit by the worst tragedy in the history of the RNLI has a litany of hilarious tales to relate.

The Lytham St Annes lifeboat house perches on the edge of the River Ribble estuary at Lytham Green. It lies roughly opposite the very spot across the bay where the world's first lifeboat station was established at Formby around 1776. A seaborne emergency service was sorely needed off this coast, due to a combination of heavy sea traffic heading for Preston and other ports, the dawn of popular seaside holidays and venomous tidal races over the dangerous sandbanks of the River Ribble.

When the schooner *British Token* was being wrecked on the night of 24 November 1856, the master formally addressed his crew thus: 'You must prepare for either Hell or Heaven before morning, because we are on those infernal Ribble Banks.'

Three crew survived, one drowned.

On 9 December 1886, a 491-ton, 3-masted barque the *Mexico* ran aground on a sandbank between Southport and Lytham St Annes. A gale was gusting up to force nine and the captain of the *Mexico* signalled his distress as the crew lashed themselves to the mizzen mast rigging and hoped for the best. The fore and main masts had been chopped down to reduce windage. The signals were spotted almost simultaneously in St Annes, which had its own boat at the time, and Southport. Both lifeboats were launched, to be joined by the Lytham boat. It was the latter boat which reached the *Mexico*, almost on its beam ends in furious seas, and with great difficulty, rescued the crew of twelve by the eerie light of a full moon. The other two lifeboats were swallowed by the storm.

In all, 27 lifeboatmen died to save 12 strangers. And 16 widows and 50 orphans were left grieving. The disaster touched the heart of the nation and assisted the start of a public tradition of giving to the RNLI. Queen Victoria and the German Kaiser made handsome donations, and over £30,000 were raised for the dependants in a few weeks – a huge sum in those days. A sombre and compelling statue was erected on the promenade at St Annes, of a lifeboatman in sou'wester and cork jacket looking towards the scene of the disaster on the far side of the estuary. Generations of holidaymakers have gazed silently at this very effective reminder of the sacrifices lifeboatmen are prepared to make.

And still do. The *Mexico* disaster still casts its shadow, but the men who run the combined Lytham St Annes boat today exhibit a distinctive Northern sense of humour – possibly an antidote to some of the fatal incidents they have all witnessed. Men such as Arthur Wignall, a cox from 1970 until his retirement in 1988; Frank Kilroy, the honorary secretary; Tony West, currently second cox and mechanic; David Forshaw, head launcher and author of the station's history; and Arnold Broxup, former head launcher with twenty-four years' service. When this group get together to relate their experiences it is this humour which bubbles to the surface in a series of collectively told stories.

The one clearly most often related concerns the plight of a certain gentleman, now dead, who manned – totally on his own – a navigation barge, built as a tug in 1898, called the *Musgrave*, which was moored out in the Ribble Estuary only three-quarters of a mile from the lifeboat station. A colourful character, his job was to monitor the ships going up to Preston, informing the dock officials by landline telephone to prepare berths and alert tugs, if necessary. He was known in Lytham for his partiality for a certain brand of beer. On the night of 15 January 1954, he apparently took a measure of ale to ward off the bitter cold, sculled his small punt across to the *Musgrave* and went to bed.

'He got out his bunk during the night to attend to a call of nature, and stepped into two feet of water. That had a very sobering effect. There was a force eight gale blowing and someone had left a porthole open. He soon realised the *Musgrave* was sinking, but not all was lost – he still had his telephone. And it was working. He dialled 999 and got one of those formal operators who calmly asked for his name, address and telephone number and which service he wanted. "Never mind that," he yelled. "Send the bloody lifeboat quick. I'm sinking!"

'It took a little time to clear up the confusion, and the lifeboat was launched with Joe Parkinson, cox at the time, at the helm.

'But when we arrived at the scene we couldn't find the *Musgrave*. We were going up and down with the searchlight looking everywhere when suddenly someone shouted "There he is!"

'The *Musgrave* had gone down, but about ten feet of mast was sticking out of the water. And he was clinging to the top of it! He was fortunate the barge had gone straight down instead of turning over, but he must have had some guts to climb up because his hands were ripped to pieces by shards of rusty metal on the mast.

'So there he was, clad in his nightshirt shouting, "Hurry up, will you!" He began climbing down, but we had to ask him to go back because we were afraid the lifeboat would crush him. He didn't think much of that. Anyway, Joe managed to manoeuvre alongside and we snatched him in.

'There was a sequel to this tale. The man was obviously suffering from the cold, so George Harrison, one of the crew, brought a bottle of rum from the stores. You are not supposed to do this unless you are at least three miles off and have been out for more than two hours. But George considered this an emergency, and on the way back about half the bottle went into our casualty before we got him ashore to the ambulance. It made him very happy.

'One of the senior nurses at the hospital lived next door to George and when she saw him the morning afterwards she declared: "What were you trying to do to that poor man – kill him? We had to pump all that rum out of his stomach before we could treat him for hypothermia and shock."

'He was grateful though. Left us £100 in his will.

'There was another notable occasion when a French boat from Bayonne ran aground with a cargo of sulphur. Sparks began to fly from the hull so the lifeboat launched to stand by and, if necessary, take off the crew, which had panicked somewhat and indicated a keen desire to abandon ship. But the captain threatened them with his revolver and ordered them to remain on board. He had put the anchor out and said the boat would refloat on the tide. He went ashore himself twice to organise things, but his crew didn't. The vessel came free as he predicted and our crew went aboard for a farewell breakfast. And then the tragedy happened. As we were leaving, he said he had a bottle of the best Napoleon brandy for us and tossed it to one of the crewmen – who dropped it. There were tears in the eyes of our crew as they saw that brandy swilling around the scuppers.'

The Lytham St Annes station has also been afflicted recently by disappearing lifeboats. Their craft is anchored about a third of a mile away out in the estuary and in a thick fog one November they couldn't find it for a very long time. Fortunately it wasn't an urgent service. But there was a much more dramatic occasion as the honorary secretary, Frank Kilroy, recalls with a certain wryness.

'I had only been appointed three months when, in January 1991, a crew member rang me early one morning to say that the boat had gone. There had been a force eleven and a huge tide during the night, and the boat was nowhere to be seen. So I had to ring up the RNLI headquarters to tell them that their new secretary had lost their boat. It was not a good moment.

'I rang the coastguards to inform them and was on the point of asking for a helicopter to stand by when the phone rang. It was a rural policeman from the village of Freckleton, four miles up the river. He said that Farmer Braithwaite had found a blue and orange boat in his top field, and was it anything to do with us?

'It took us three weeks to retrieve it. We hired a barge with a winch and an ex-army tractor lorry to drag it back to the river. Strangely, the boat didn't have a mark on it.'

Of course there is the other side of the coin. There was the occasion in 1981 when they were having a carnival day for the lifeboat, with beach activities, a funfair, the inshore boat doing simulated rescues and a helicopter hovering around. The weather had been so bad that the event was almost cancelled in the morning. During the festivities a report came through that a red flare had been spotted. It turned out to be a yacht that had been foolhardy enough to leave the Isle of Man for the mainland despite severe weather forecasts. Fortunately for the lone crewman, the Lytham St Annes lifeboat was fully crewed and ready to go immediately. As it turned out, another fifteen minutes would have been fatal.

Coxswain Wignall had to risk entering shallow water in a force eight to get to the yacht, which at first appeared to have been abandoned. But as they came around her they saw a man clinging to the stern and so wrapped up in his own lifeline that he could neither reboard his boat nor reach his inflatable dinghy being towed astern. Assistant mechanic Brian Pearson leaped into the dinghy, aiming to cut him free with an axe. But the yacht and its dinghy then swung around opposite sides of the lifeboat's bow, threatening to crush the man. So Brian jumped into the water and pulled him away, whilst crewman Bob Kennedy boarded the yacht, cut the line and dragged him into the yacht. Brian was helped back into the lifeboat.

But the problems were far from over. A rope from the yacht had fouled the lifeboat's port propeller, stalling the engine. There was no time to try and clear it since Bob Kennedy and the yachtsman were still on board the yacht which was being blown into even shallower water. With considerable skill, Arthur Wignall turned the lifeboat on its one remaining engine and, knowing he only had one chance, drove straight on to the yacht's side. Both men were taken off as she sank. Even then the lifeboat was at serious risk, because it could not go astern against the wind and tide with a single engine. So it had to go ahead again and turn in shallow water, a perilous but unavoidable manoeuvre, and the boat bumped against the seabed before coming around successfully into deeper water.

The yachtsman survived hypothermia, and bronze medals were awarded to Arthur Wignall and Brian Pearson. Bob Kennedy was presented with a vellum, a certificate commending a courageous deed which ranks just below a bronze medal.

In June of 1994, the infernal banks of the Ribble demonstrated their savagery yet again when a thirty-six-foot ferro-concrete motor sailer went aground on the marsh banks. The Lytham St Annes men had been impressed by the vessel as it progressed down the estuary.

'It looked as if it could sail anywhere in the world, and would just lie snugly on the bank until it refloated. But a wind piped up and with the flood tide the waves began to pound it. The owner said he heard a noise, looked down and saw water at the bottom of the engine. He just had time to get off a Mayday. Within three minutes his boat was falling apart.

'There were three of them in the water, including a girl who couldn't swim at all, and they just had buoyancy aids, not proper life jackets. So Arthur Wignall's son, Russell, went into the water and got the girl into the yacht's dinghy. But that capsized. Anyway, he managed to save her and the inshore boat pulled them both out. Russell was given a medal by the *Daily Star* for that.

'We went down the next day and it was a remarkable sight. Eleven tons of concrete littered around, and a lot of chicken wire!'

For people who are thrown into the sea, the time of year is vital. In winter hypothermia can kill you within the hour, but in summer a person stands a much better chance of survival, particularly if he or she has a protective layer of body fat.

Four young men from Liverpool set off from Formby in a seventeen-foot speedboat for a day's fishing one July morning, and it tipped over. One swam for eleven hours and made it ashore. Another was found by the Lytham St Annes crew floating in two life jackets, semi-conscious. He had been in the water for over twenty hours, but he weighed over twenty stones. It took four men to lift him into the lifeboat, and he survived. The bodies of the other two were washed up at Blackpool the following week.

Another man who had a bizarre, long distance experience in the Ribble Estuary began his adventure on Southport beach. What happened next could have been lifted straight from the script of a broad Northern comedy at any Blackpool theatre. The sea is generally reluctant to come anywhere near the promenade at Southport and visitors wishing to bathe face a considerable walk. The man in question announced his intention to do just that to his wife, sitting with her knitting on a deckchair, and set off. Some time later men on a sand dredger in the river heard shouting in the water. It was the bather from Southport, who had been whipped away towards Lytham by the tidal wave. They hauled him out and the lifeboat came to bring him ashore. Since he had nothing to wear but his swimming trunks the police drove him back to Southport beach, where his wife was still in the deckchair, knitting away unconcernedly. And when he told her he had been to Lytham, she berated him soundly for trying to deceive her!

There was another favourite story told by the merry men of the Lytham St Annes crew. Sometimes their sense of humour has a distinct Northern bluntness which was colourfully demonstrated when they rescued a windsurfer being carried off by the tide one blustery New Year's Eve. He was prone on the board, totally exhausted, and clearly far from young. When they questioned him he admitted he was sixty-five so they chided him for being daft enough to go out in bad weather at his age. He then said he had been given the windsurfer by his wife as a Christmas present.

'Aye, and I'll bet she's at home right now going through the insurance policies,' was the ironic comment of a crewman not noted for tact and diplomacy.

Of all the seagoing playthings the public brings to the northwest coast, cheap inflatables are the major cause of emergencies. An unnoticed change of tide, or a sudden squall, and a child can be snatched away to oblivion.

However, there are two young boys who have entered the folklore of the Lytham St Annes lifeboatmen, and their tale has a happy and remarkable ending. Only around seven years of age, they had launched a tiny inflatable up the river towards Preston and were spotted floating down towards the estuary and the open sea. The inshore lifeboat intercepted them in time and brought them ashore. They had a small suitcase with them. Apparently quite unconcerned, they deflated their boat, politely asked for the use of a hosepipe and washed it down. Under the astounded gaze of the crewmen, they neatly folded it and placed it in the suitcase.

Then they calmly carried it to a bus stop and caught the next bus home!

5

Hell and High Water

It began with a sound like distant thunder, welling up from the middle of a heaving, boozing, singing mass of humanity in the pub. And it signalled that the patience of the men of Cadgwith Cove had finally snapped.

It had been planned as the day of days in the cove, but it had gone horribly and inexplicably wrong. The weather in the rest of the country was positively tropical, but Cornwall had been hit by an Atlantic storm. The barbecue had floated away, the brass band had gone home and, worst of all, the gig races against all comers had been cancelled. No boat could venture out in such conditions.

But with a roar of frustration, the men of Cadgwith Cove surged out into the stinging rain and – like picking up a matchbox – swept up *Buller*, their brand-new thirty-two-foot racing gig, and went ahead with the launch they had planned for the big day. Against all considered advice they ploughed into a sea made furious by an easterly which had been gusting to force eight only hours before.

They would be denied no longer. The village had waited seventy years for the moment – the launch of the long-awaited replacement to their last racing boat, which had been smashed by a freak cliff fall.

The sea fought back, and two or three received gashes they would bear for weeks as they struggled to control the craft. It would rear up six feet and then slam down into flesh and bone. In less capable hands the gig would have been reduced to driftwood. But then oars began dipping in unison as six men rowed with a power born of sheer determination and the virgin gig shot with astonishing speed through the surf, and disappeared into the mist.

Dripping people packing the shingled beach, who moments before had been muttering among themselves about the madness of it all, howled their appreciation. But the key members of the debutante crew were familiar with putting out a boat in such conditions as they were mostly members of the Lizard lifeboat, stationed a mile or two down the coast. And they were prepared to take the risk since they were hellbent on establishing their reputation in the rapidly growing sport of gig racing along the southwest coast, anxious to pit their skill and strength in their blue and white nautical greyhound, with the name *Buller* writ large across the bows – a name which could give them an inspirational edge.

To understand why, you need to appreciate the nature of Cadgwith Cove, a place with a winter population of less than 400. They are not as privileged as other Cornish fishermen, who have their boats conveniently lifted each day by the tide. For generations, Cadgwith boats had to be launched by sweat, and rolled on logs into the sea by the co-operative effort of strong men.

They also tended to fish as a team, using an ancient communal winch to get back up the beach with their catch. It was a system which threw up a leader who made the decisions of the day.

Such a man was Richard Redvers Arthur, born on the day in 1899 that General Sir Redvers Buller attempted to relieve Ladysmith in the Boer War. Nearly everyone has a nickname in the cove, so Buller it was. He was a celebrated repository of Cornish folklore and songs, and his reputation spread throughout the Duchy. When he died at the age of eighty-one, six Cadgwith men, a gig crew naturally, carried Buller a very long mile along steeply winding lanes to his grave. Occasionally, one would yield the honour to a selected representative from the enormous crowd.

Like all true Cadgwith men, Buller hunted shellfish for a living, risked his neck in the local lifeboat as a duty, and raced gigs for pleasure. Pilot gigs are part of Cornish history, and they evolved their greyhound shape from sheer necessity. When the clippers of old came in sight of land, they needed a local pilot to guide them through the hazardous rocks to the safety of harbour. The first boat alongside got the job and the money. Similarly, if a vessel was driven by storms to destruction and abandoned to the Cornish wreckers, the fastest gig got the pick of the spoils.

The men of Cadgwith were historically among the finest gig racers – sometimes unbeatable and always feared. But one day around 1916, a gale brought down part of the cliff above the boathouse and their precious craft, the *Rose*, was shattered beyond repair. Until the arrival of the *Buller* they had been obliged to borrow gigs.

Their £8,500 new gig had been built, in the traditional manner, of well-matured Cornish narrow-leafed elm – much to the satisfaction of men like Sharkey Stevens, who took over the leadership from Buller by common consent, and veteran gigmen like the pugnacious Plugger Jane and 'Pedro' José, who was reputedly descended from a survivor of the Spanish Armada washed up in the cove. That memorable launch day calmed down eventually into a reasonable evening and the sea became sufficiently benign for *Buller* to be launched again with a privileged guest or two aboard. One of the first was Spider Bewes, a Cadgwith Cover by inclination, otherwise known as Rodney Bewes, one of the famous Likely Lads.

They were not all impressed in the cove by his television fame, but when he spent months crabbing across to the Scillies and Brittany with them he was accepted into their lives. Nicknamed affectionately after the most useless crab a pot can yield, Spider had flown in from Los Angeles the night before especially to attend the launch.

Since then, the *Buller* has been joined by a sister gig, named *Rose* after the boat that perished, and the Cadgwith men are usually among the front runners during the summer weekend gig races.

The passing years have changed some of the Cove's traditions. The old winch has been largely supplanted by a tractor, which means that boats can be launched independently instead of the fishermen being obliged to work as a group. Built in 1911 (they once had to fend off an American visitor who wanted to buy it and take it home), the winch is still maintained in immaculate order under the supervision of the Cove's elder statesmen, particularly Sharkey Stevens, who, now nearing seventy, has retired from fishing. He still spends much time in the narrow harbour, ready to assist if bad weather and big tides combine with the wrong wind direction to send the sea roaring into the village street. When that happens, all traffic stops as boats are dragged to safety up the hill out of the cove.

Even that precaution is not sufficient sometimes, as Sharkey recalls.

'It was so bad once that the road was completely torn up and my boat was flung into a house, cracking the wall!'

Sharkey acquired his nickname ('My real name is a secret – don't like it, don't know what my mother was thinking about!') in his twenties when he took a visitor fishing in an eighteen-foot boat and harpooned a twenty-foot basking shark.

'I expected it to charge off in a forward direction, but it decided to go around in circles and wrap the harpoon rope around the propeller of the engine, which was only three horsepower. Then it dived deep and still went around in circles. The rope was tangled up everywhere. It was a bit worrying at first but we managed to pull him up eventually and sort out the rope. It took a long time, though.'

Since his father, Ernest, was cox of the Lizard lifeboat, Sharkey naturally chose to accompany him rather than join the Cadgwith boat. At the time he was sixteen and officially too young to be a lifeboatman but the Second World War had started two years earlier and manpower was short. Their thirty-five-footer was called the *Guide of Dunkirk* to commemorate the part that it had played in that immortal evacuation of the British Army from France in 1940, and had been shot up in the process.

'We had several incidents off the Lizard during the war. Once we went to pick up a couple of German aircrew after their bomber had been shot down by one of our fighters. We took a Boer War veteran with us who was in the Home Guard and armed with a revolver. We found that one of the Germans was already dead, shot in the neck, when we arrived but the other one was still in the water and shouting for help. Whereupon this *Dad's Army* man drew his revolver, pointed it at the German and bawled, "Don't start bloody shouting here – you weren't shouting just now when you were bombing Wales!" The man was terrified. Even I thought he was going to blow his head off.

'There was another occasion during the war when we nearly got our own heads blown off, partly due to our own fault. A cargo boat in a convoy had been torpedoed and sunk off the Lizard by a German submarine. When we arrived the survivors had already been picked up by one of the other boats in the convoy and there was a destroyer racing around dropping depth charges to try and get the submarine. Must have sunk it, too, because plenty of oil rose to the surface. Trouble was the destroyer nearly blew us out of the water with those depth charges going off all over the place. Anyway it made off, and everything went peaceful again when we came across a big circular float about four feet high and the same in width, painted red. Don't ask me why, but one of the crew slapped an axe into it.

'It went off with a hell of a great roar. Ten feet of flames and smoke which scorched the oars on the side of the lifeboat, and it was sheer luck that no one was hurt. The thing was a phosphorous smokeboat used to lay down smokescreens and within minutes everything around was blotted out. It went on for a long time and I thought that my old man, the cox, would get the sack when it was reported. Apparently no one said a thing and he got away with it.'

Sharkey nominated the astonishing episode of the *Flying Enterprise* as the most celebrated mission during his time on the Lizard lifeboat. The Dutch skipper of the boat, Captain Kurt Carlsen, became a world-famous figure as a result. He had sailed from Hamburg in December 1951, bound for New York with a cargo of Volkswagen cars, pig iron and antiques, as well as thirty-nine American seamen and ten German passengers. The 7,000-ton vessel was hit by a force ten hurricane and it was necessary to put out a Mayday and abandon ship off the Lizard. But Captain Kurt, dubbed 'The Flying Dutchman', stayed on board – alone. The ship turned on its side and still he stayed, with a US destroyer and a tug from Falmouth standing by. The drama went on for days and newspapers around the globe ran front-page stories of the 'Captain Courageous' variety.

The captain was a man of few words, and declined to explain why he chose to remain. There were rumours of a secret cargo of gold bullion and at least one group of local Cornish divers contemplated trying to locate the wreck, because the *Flying Enterprise* did sink as it was taken under tow. Carlsen stepped off the funnel, which was horizontal to the water, and swam to a rescue boat.

As the world marvelled at his courage and daring, others more closely connected with the drama had slightly different views, including Sharkey Stevens, who stood by with the Lizard lifeboat for four days.

'We were a bit fed up with him really. We had put out at four o'clock in the morning, travelled thirty miles and stayed there for eighteen hours on the first day. As a matter of fact, he was quite comfortable even though the ship was on its side. We were having more trouble than him with the bad weather. We kept asking him over the radio to come off but he wouldn't speak to us. Pathé News came out to film him for the cinema newsreels and we earned six quid from them. On the last day we were running out of fuel and had to return to Falmouth. As we were halfway there he decided he wanted to come off and asked us to return, but we couldn't. The Cadgwith boat was launched but he had already been rescued by the tug before they got there.' Sharkey served for about fifteen years altogether with the Lizard lifeboat and then joined the Cadgwith crew – Buller was the second cox – for the final four years of its illustrious history. It was wound up in 1962 and the boathouse is now the home for the Cadgwith gigs.

Unlike some of the other small, isolated Cornish coastal communities, Cadgwith is remarkably tolerant towards strangers, unless you wish to interfere with certain time-honoured traditions. There is a legend in the cove – where the smuggling of brandy and silks in the old days was an integral part of the local economy and several houses still have secret compartments – that one revenue man's life came to a fearful end in Cadgwith.

'It's a story told to old men by their fathers,' said Sharkey. 'They killed him outside the pub, so they say.'

Shipwrecked mariners were obviously treated differently, even those washed up from the Spanish Armada, which had tried to conquer England. The ancestor of Parry 'Pedro' José, a popular Cover and member of the original *Buller* gig crew, may have arrived there in such a manner. It is impossible to prove either way. But one legend is surely based on fact since it is in the memory of the parents of those living today.

Apparently, a man turned up in the cove some years before the turn of the century and indicated a desire to stay. How he communicated this can only be guessed at, because he was both deaf and dumb. Of large physique and enormous strength, he was allowed to become a member of the community.

They called him Dummer. Although it is said they occasionally played some cruel tricks on him they gave him food and shelter. He made his home in a sail loft.

Bert Wyley, born in 1902 and perhaps the cove's oldest resident, who served in the old sailing lifeboat, heard the stories about Dummer from those who knew him.

'He died about 1900, so I never knew him personally. But I heard he was a very big man and very popular around here. No one knew where he came from but he was a fisherman and could make beautiful lobster pots.'

To this day, the place where this poor, strange and vulnerable man lived out his days in Cadgwith is known as 'Dummer's Loft'.

6

The Last Place in England

There is another Cornish cove which, like Cadgwith, is situated close to one of the furthest-flung promontories in the land. The Lizard is the most southerly place in Britain, but its sister peninsula, just a few miles to the west, is more celebrated: Land's End.

Just round the corner from this seasonally crowded extremity, a small community crouches beneath a tall cliff which denies them the benefit of the sun during winter. This is the price they have to pay for the limited shelter the looming granite provides, for this is the last place in England, and none is more cruelly exposed to the brutality of the sea: Sennen Cove.

When the northwesterlies blow – and they do with harsh regularity – there is no protection for Sennen Cove, and men have died trying merely to secure their boats on the slipway. Living in this manner, generation after generation, has evolved a particularly fierce breed of men, almost tribal in their insularity. Cornwall is known for the barriers it can erect to oblige outsiders to keep their distance, but even the most defensive of them hold the inhabitants of Sennen Cove in awe. And with distinct disapproval in certain cases. They certainly do not regard them as blood brothers.

It must be emphasised that this applies to the Sennen Covers, not the inhabitants of Sennen Village which clusters well above the cliff around the road to Land's End. They are known in the cove as 'Over-Hillers' and used traditionally to be detested. It's different now, of course, but in the distant past a young 'Over-Hiller', a farmer's son, was supposedly put to death for daring to woo the daughter of a Cover. There was an echo of this bitter division as recently as the Second World War when a Sennen man, serving in the forces, turned up in Bombay to be told that another Sennen man was also in the city. It was assumed that he would be eager for a meeting, since the entire population of the Sennen area wouldn't fill a 747 aeroplane. But when the newly arrived man discovered the identity of his fellow Sennenite, he coldly declined.

Legend also says they had a particularly severe way in Sennen of dealing with revenue men. In Cadgwith, it was a quick death outside the pub. At Sennen Cove they apparently buried the wretch up to his neck at the low-water mark and waited for the tide to come in.

There is something else which is special to Sennen Cove – something that even less than ten years ago would touch an exposed nerve throughout the entire community. It concerned a particular fish which once swarmed profitably into their bay – the grey mullet.

At one time very recently – and this is no exaggeration – for an outsider to even mention the word 'mullet' in the cove would create open hostility. For this desirable fish once led to the nearest thing to civil war in Cornwall since Oliver Cromwell hung up his helmet.

To Cornish fishermen, the mullet is a wonderful fish. When it appears, it does so in enormous numbers, bunching together in a huge shoal, the combined weight of which could exceed 100 tons. Once they swarmed each year into three or four Cornish coves, and the largest shoal traditionally turned up in Sennen Cove. Catching them was a communal affair, and each of the favoured places invested in a seine net big enough to encompass the dome of St Paul's. The one in Sennen was so heavy that it required fifty men to carry it to the boat.

The net would be stealthily placed around the shoal by boat, and then hauled in by a line of men on the beach. It was an exciting, frenzied scene full of clamour and sweat as muscles were stretched to the limit with men in the boat trying to beat back the fish attempting to escape the net, for they were not called the leaping grey mullet for nothing.

Often the shoals would be watched from the cliffs at Sennen for days until they moved into a favourable position far enough away from rocks for the men to pounce. Tension would build in the cove, and strangers would be scarcely tolerated. Even 'outsiders' who had lived in the cove for years knew they must stay away. One such resident, who was an official of the Sennen lifeboat, said there had been several mullet catches during his time in residence but he had never witnessed the spectacle because he knew he must not venture near the beach at mullet time.

It was around one of those particular times when a group of five men from Par, another fishing village further along the Cornish coast, turned up along the road above Sennen. They were mobile fishermen, tracking along the coast one Sunday in the early sixties with their nets and associated gear trailing behind their Land Rover, looking for fishing opportunities. They spotted a 'lovely little bunch of mullet' and they followed it along the coast until it joined the main shoal, which they estimated weighed sixty tons. And the place where that happened was – ominously – Sennen Cove. A member of the group recalled what happened next.

'We stopped, and went to get the net and go down to the beach when we spotted about thirty men coming down towards us. At first we thought they were just people out for a Sunday afternoon walk, but when they got nearer we realised they were fishermen.

'Well, what they weren't going to do to us . . . We just cannot repeat what they said. One of the younger ones took out a knife and said he would slash our necks to pieces, heave our boat over the rocks and out to sea, and then he would go up the hill and have our vehicle tipped over the cliff. He did start by cutting a few meshes out of our net and the footropes. But then one of our party, who was nearly seventy, got a bit heated up, seized the anchor and said that if that man cut the net any more he would beat him over the head with it.

'So he stopped, and then told us that if we dared to put our net around that shoal of mullet all our gear would have fetched up on the Longships Lighthouse, and we along with it.

'I was frightened out of my wits. I am convinced that if it had been a hundred years ago they would have hanged us on the spot.'

A slightly different version of that encounter is told by the Sennen men, who say that the old man didn't threaten anyone with an anchor but said that the net hadn't been paid for. So, apart from having their trailer turned over, there was no further trouble and they were allowed to beat a hasty retreat.

But that was not the end of the matter, not by any means. The pride of the men of Par had been mortally offended, and they determined to redress the matter in the most basic way. The confrontation that followed between the two communities has been embroidered down the years in Cornish folklore. Some people believe that firearms were readied on both sides, others that the army had to be stood by. Most of those involved are reluctant to go into detail, but there is no doubt that it was a very serious incident which, but for the skilful handling on the part of the police, could have had disastrous consequences.

Derek Chappell, who was a policeman for thirty years, including a spell as the lone upholder of the law in Sennen Cove, reckons that up to fifty policemen were deployed when the Par men returned in strength to Sennen.

'They had to be brought in from several stations in the area. I don't know how many men from Par were on the move but three or four lorries carrying fishing gear turned up and a lot more came in private cars. The men of Sennen came up the hill, armed with what they could find, such as pick handles and knives, I understand. There was no sign of any firearms but I suppose they may have had some hidden. That was the first occasion, which was the worst. The Par men got to the lower car park in Sennen and I am sure if they had got out their nets to try and go for the mullet which were still there but among the rocks where it wasn't possible to shoot, it would have led to their nets being all cut, boats smashed and general fighting. It was clear a riot was a strong possibility. But they all probably realised that no mullet would be caught that day and with tact and good humour we managed to separate them and get the Par men up to the car park at the top of the hill, still complaining they had every right to go for the fish. Then they were persuaded to go home.

'Then about two or three weeks later, with the mullet still massing but remaining in the wrong place, we received information that the Par men were on the move again. This time we were well prepared, and we put up roadblocks to stop them from reaching the cove and managed once again to talk them out of it.

'Ironically, that mullet shoal stayed amongst the rocks and eventually broke up and headed out to sea. So nobody had them!'

The Par men, who vividly recall 'one great big Superintendent', who loudly announced that he would personally put behind bars the first man to start trouble, are still indignant about the incident.

'The Sennen men seem to think that any fish that comes into their bay is theirs. The St Ives and the St Just men would tell you the same, and they once frightened the life out of some French fishermen who came into the bay, by throwing rocks down on to their boats from the cliff.'

The Covers stoutly defend their claim to exclusive rights in their bay. Maurice Hutchins, coxswain of the Sennen lifeboat for twelve years until he retired in 1990, is very clear about it.

'If we are going to allow other people to come in and catch the mullet – our traditional amount – then it's taking part of our living, isn't it? If you can't keep what's yours in your own community you may as well pack up first as last.'

The late Cecil Roberts was even more emphatic on the subject. He was one of those in the Sennen ranks who prepared to do battle. He colourfully described the event as 'a bit of a mutiny'.

'You have to stand your own ground, don't you? We're not going to see foreigners coming in and taking the food out of our mouths. And they didn't come under that hill!'

Cecil Roberts had one of the highest public profiles along the Land's End peninsula – an area thick on the ground with characters looking as though they had stepped out of the pages of a Robert Louis Stevenson novel. Cecil cut an impressive figure in his old age, as he sat, lavishly bewhiskered, on a seat overlooking Sennen harbour, growling at over-inquisitive tourists and threatening them with his stick if they pointed a camera at him. And yet those same strangers would fall over themselves to offer him a pint in the State House pub at Land's End.

He would proceed regularly to this haven on the back of one of the donkeys that he kept, threading a perilous route along the cliff top from Sennen, thus attracting much attention. It was rumoured that he was once able to drink all one winter without paying a penny because so many pints had been left 'in the pump' for him during the season.

Cecil lived in a venerable thatched cottage which had been the family home for generations. His grandmother was certainly born there and probably her grandmother. The appointments made few concessions to the twentieth century. Not even electricity intruded and he shared the place with a dog and nine cats.

Naturally, he was a member of the Sennen lifeboat crew, rising to deputy cox. He took part in many dramatic rescues – the Sennen boat has saved over 300 lives since it was formed in 1853 – and talked rather wistfully about the lack of wrecks in his later years.

'No, you don't get the wrecks like you used to now they've got this radar and things. We sometimes get a lot of fog in the summer and in the old days there would be a steamboat or two ashore without doubt. Nowadays, they know where they are because of all these implements they have aboard. The days of the Cornish Wrecker have long gone, never to return.'

Cecil could recall wrecks going back to 1913, when a three-masted barque from Sweden ran ashore one Sunday morning on the top beach at Sennen.

'Ground sea like hills there was. In ten minutes she was all level . . . went to pieces, everything gone. She was carrying a cargo of firebricks and coal. A lot of hen houses in Sennen were built from the firebricks and the coal was lovely to burn in the house. Handsome!'

Cecil was descended from a long line of Cornish Wreckers – not, it must be stressed, those who deliberately lured ships to their doom, but men who went to harvest what they could from the abandoned vessels after first trying to save the crew. And wrecking could have fatal consequences, too, as Cecil recalled.

'My grandfather was killed going out with four other men to the wreck of the *Malta*, which went aground in fog near Cape Cornwall in 1886. They loaded their fishing boat with general cargo, but not satisfied with that they took a boat from the *Malta* and filled that up, too. Coming back under sail they were passing a shoal of rock called Great Ledge and a big sea hit them. The other four were picked up, but the boat they were towing was turned over and broke my grandfather's neck.

'Two more in my family were lost around 1921. They went out herring fishing one Friday morning. The herring were plentiful and they overloaded the boat. A strong breeze came up from the southeast and there was so much weight that the boat sunk under them and they were drowned.'

It is indisuptable that a typical Sennen Cover has to come to terms with the high level of risk involved in earning a living in the traditional manner. And the shouldering of responsibility in the lifeboat crew, as most young Covers yearn to do, is a question of honour and pride – the two prime factors in the character of Sennen folk.

Maurice Hutchins is a Sennen Cover born and bred, and spent his boyhood around the harbour, eagerly looking after the punts which ferried the men to their boats and occasionally being rewarded with a chance to go fishing with them. That's how he learned the basic skills of seamanship. A child of the thirties, he fished to supplement the table at home whilst the men would hunt rabbits on the moors to reduce the butcher's bill. Summers were comparatively benevolent because the weather usually allowed the time and opportunity to pursue the fish at distances which would have been unwise in winter. Maurice left school at fourteen, served an apprenticeship as a carpenter, did his National Service and came back to the cove to volunteer for the lifeboat whilst still working at his trade – a familiar route for budding Covers, and Maurice made it to the top quite unexpectedly in 1978, when the cox, Eric Pengilley, died suddenly at the age of fifty-three.

'We had a meeting to decide who to nominate as a successor, and the honorary secretary put my name forward. But before it went any further I said I wanted to hear if anyone else wanted to be considered, and insisted that every member of the crew should say his piece. By then I had started fishing out of Newlyn for a living. It was reasonably lucrative, and it's not easy to give up a job to go to one which pays less. It's a lot different now, but at the time the wage for a cox was around fifty pounds a week, which was within a fiver of a local tradesman's rate.

'Anyway, they voted for me unanimously so I said that I would agree on condition that I could go fishing during the summer to supplement my income, always providing I could find a deputy to stand in for me if necessary. The RNLI were more flexible in those days, and my proposal was accepted. Considering the twenty-four-hour-a-day responsibility, the wage then just wasn't enough, but since that time there has been a big shake-up right across the board and pay and pensions have been much improved. I don't know what the pay for a cox is now, but when I retired at fifty-six five years ago I was earning well over £200 a week.

'Of course there is another side to being a lifeboatman – the deep satisfaction you feel when you have helped to save someone's life. That is worth far more than any sum of money you can make.'

Maurice and his men shared in several epic battles with the sea over the years of his leadership, most notable perhaps the night in 1981 when an Icelandic coaster with a cargo of fertiliser developed an alarming list to starboard in a southwesterly about five miles off Land's End.

By the time the Sennen lifeboat had reached the scene a

rescue helicopter had taken off three men, but the sea conditions were so bad that the helicopter winchman had been hurt as he snatched them to safety. To continue with that method would have put his life at serious risk. Another eight men were still on board, so the lifeboat moved in. Two life rafts had been launched at the rear of the stricken vessel and as the lifeboat approached one man at a time would jump on to a raft.

'All the time we were going in and out, the helicopter hovered overhead, following our every move and illuminating the sea with its powerful light. Since it was pitch-black that was invaluable, a very high order of co-operation.

'We picked up three men from the raft. Another two missed and fell into the drink but we managed to fish them out. That left three remaining on board so we went close to the vessel and signalled them to come to the stern where I thought I could get the nose of the lifeboat close enough for them to jump on. It was a bit hairy manoeuvring in close quarters because everything was moving around a bit. The lifeboat sustained some damage, but we took another two off. That left the skipper, traditionally the last man to leave. His boat was very low in the water by then, and a big sea almost submerged her so I steamed in expecting that he would be washed overboard. But when we came close we saw he was still there, and just then the helicopter came in front of us and dropped the winch wire straight on to his chest, he grabbed it, and was hoisted rapidly to safety. So between us we got the lot off.'

For that exploit, Maurice was awarded the RNLI silver medal and his crew received Certificates of Service. But what really pleased him was the reaction of the people of Iceland.

'Their government gave each of my crew and the helicopter crew a silver medal which I thought was marvellous. We were the first foreigners to win it, and the President of Iceland, a lady, came to England especially to present them.

'Eleven man saved, eleven medals awarded – very symbolic.'

Valour is the word inscribed on the RNLI medals, but Maurice steadfastly refuses to accept that he is an acknowledged hero, like so many who have served in the British lifeboats.

'Yes, I know the public thinks all lifeboatmen are heroes, but it's not always the case. I don't know what a hero is.

'I certainly ain't a hero!'

There are at least seven people alive and well in Iceland today who would strenuously contest that statement.

7

Triple Crew Copper

Derek Chappell must have a unique record in the history of the RNLI. For thirty years he was a policeman, and yet he managed to serve in three lifeboats – Sennen Cove, Penlee and St Ives. Two happened by pure chance, but he was a regular member of Sennen and is extremely proud of being a three crew copper.

He was born in 1933 in Newlyn, the West Country's principal fishing port, son of a Great Western Railway man, and went to sea after leaving school. He engaged in long lining, trawling and driving pilchard before he was called to do his National Service in the navy. But he became disillusioned on his return.

'I joined a boat which was paying off debts from former trips, so I decided to quit and apply to join the police force. I passed all the exams but the Devon and Cornwall Constabulary told me I was half an inch short of the five foot eleven minimum height, so I was rejected. However, the Metropolitan Police accepted me. I trained at Hendon and served in Chelsea. The World's End pub was on my beat, and then I ended up at Land's End, which must be another sort of record. You see, I applied for a transfer to Cornwall, got an interview with the Chief Constable who just asked two or three questions before announcing that I was now a member of the Cornwall Constabulary. He told me the missing half-inch didn't matter any more – he was just delighted to get a trained officer from London at no expense to his force!'

Derek eventually became the sole Sennen Cove copper, moving into the police house at the top of the hill, with his wife, Mary, who was a teacher doing supply work, and their infant son. Another child was born to them in Sennen. Derek had a big patch, stretching from Lamorna Cove, across Sancreed to the other side of the tiny St Just airport, which included all the coast. His transport to begin with was a 250 cc motorcycle which sometimes failed to make the steep hill out of Sennen Cove.

'When I took over, I was a foreigner, arriving from a foreign place though I was born just around the corner. It was very clear they were suspicious of me. Anyway, the year I arrived a Spanish vessel went down off Tatter-du, in between Land's End and Penzance, with a cargo of marine ply and shotguns. Suddenly people began to be polite and went out of their way to say "Hello", particularly in the coves near where the Spanish ship had sunk. Then I noticed sheets of plywood all over the place.

'Well . . . I had no proof about where they came from. As far as I knew, they could have been storing it ready to inform the Receiver of Wrecks. So I decided to act like Nelson and turn a blind eye. They also salvaged some very fine Spanish shotguns, beautifully decorated along the barrels and the stock.

'Anyway, from then on the new policeman had obviously been accepted.

'Then I decided to dress up the police station a bit with glass globes, fishing lines and model boats. The locals asked me what I knew about fishing, so I told them I was a fisherman out of Newlyn before I joined the force. I could talk their language.

'Next thing I had the cox of the Sennen lifeboat, Eric Pengilley, coming to introduce himself. And to my great delight he invited me to join the lifeboat crew. Now for a foreigner that was a terrific privilege.'

Derek served for over four years with the Sennen boat before they closed his station down and moved him to Penzance. It led him to a spot of bother with his superiors because the cox would inform Land's End radio that he was on the boat and they would telephone Penzance police station.

'First of all, they said I was being paid to do another job – we got one pound per launch – and that was a contravention of police rules. From the start I had told the honorary secretary that I couldn't accept the money, but he said I must have it to keep their books straight. So at the end of each season I would tot up how many trips I had done and give it back as a donation to the RNLI – duly receipted.

But I was still charged. At the hearing the Defending Officer, a chief inspector, produced all the receipts and the paperwork was stamped "No Further Action".

'Then the Chief Superintendent said: "Right, you can't go on the lifeboat any more. It's not your duty." So I said: "Sir, the primary object of a police officer is the saving of life and the protection of property. When I am out on the lifeboat that is exactly what I am trying to do." He considered this for a while and then said: "Point taken . . . Carry on in the lifeboat."'

Apart from his seamanship, Derek's training in first aid as a policeman made him a desirable candidate for any lifeboat crew, and he happened to be on the spot once when the Penlee boat was putting out on a medical call and they were one man short. He was 'thrilled to go'.

'The hat trick happened when I was in St Ives one evening with Mary, who is a local girl, and the maroons went up. We went down to watch the launch when Dan Roach, the cox at the time, leaned over the side of the boat as it was being launched and asked me to take a jacket. They were going out to a French trawler on another medical – a man had broken his leg. I cannot tell you how privileged I felt at that moment.'

It was another French trawler in trouble which led to the service which lives most vividly in Derek's mind. Not so much for the risks involved – and they were severe – but for the deep frustration with a curious Gallic attitude as well. A large vessel of around 500 tons, with a crew of more than twenty, she had broken down and was lying at anchor in very heavy seas about seven miles northwest of the Brisons, some very dangerous rocks. The anchor cable was their lifeline. If, as was very possible, it had snapped, the boat would have been driven directly on to the rocks to disaster.

'We put to sea at five minutes to midnight. It was bad and we all clipped on our lifelines. When we cleared the bay we were up to the waist in water all the time. All night long we stood by that Frenchman, fighting to keep upright ourselves. Eric Pengilley was at the helm, turning the boat continually to ride the waves – everyone shouting warnings when a big one came crashing in, everyone hanging on grimly. It was exhausting. At times like that, you have no time to be frightened, however. It's when you get back home and the wife gives you a cup of tea that your hands start shaking and you recall a particular wave and think: That could have got me.

'The amazing thing about it all was the reaction of the French crew. They wouldn't speak to us, however often we tried on the radio. We passed by flashing a light, but nothing. We saw them on the bridge but they wouldn't even wave. At about five o'clock in the morning another French trawler arrived and took it in tow. We escorted them for about ten miles before turning back, and they still refused to acknowledge us in any way whatsoever.'

Derek participated in many other, more satisfying missions with the lifeboat when grateful people were snatched from certain death. At the same time he was dealing with any crime on his patch, which was mostly petty, such as shoplifting during the busy summers. Derek himself had an Arran sweater, just knitted for him by his mother-in-law, stolen from his peg at the Sennen lifeboat house when he was out rescuing two small and terrified boys who had gone fishing from Cape Cornwall, lost their oars and started drifting out to sea.

'I couldn't bring myself to tell Mother-in-law, but after a time she said: "Don't you like that jumper I knitted you? I never see you wearing it!" So I had to confess.'

But that theft passed into insignificance when Derek investigated a sickening incident at the Penlee lifeboat house, just after the *Solomon Brown* had sunk with all hands.

'The crew's jumpers, all with their names in, were hanging on the wall. Someone came in and stole them all – dead men's clothes!

'But there was nothing really serious, no murders or violent crime when I was the Sennen policeman. Just domestic squabbles, neighbour against neighbour, and the occasional boat being cut adrift. I usually managed to sort them all out amicably. In fact, my wife arrested more people than me. For instance, early one day when I was out, three young men knocked at the door of the police house and asked Mary where they could get the ferry from Land's End. She said there were no ferries anywhere near Land's End. Then they told her they were in the army and had run away. So she arrested them.

'When I got back I found them eating my breakfast. Mary had already phoned for the Military Police to come and pick them up. So I had nothing to do with it, and no breakfast to boot!'

'On another occasion a young woman tried very hard to drown herself in Sennen Cove. It was a rough sea and it kept on throwing her back on to the beach. Four times it happened, I understand, and the waves had stripped her of all her clothes and she was badly lacerated with sandburn. She must have retrieved an old fur coat and was heading up the hill to throw herself off the cliff when she passed our police house. She saw my son in there playing, and a big fire roaring up the chimney, so she knocked on the door and asked for help. Mary was there on her own again. She saw the woman was suffering from hypothermia and put her straight into a hot bath.

'When I arrived home from patrol I made for the bathroom only to be told to stay out because there was a naked woman in the bath. Mary had taken care of everything once more, phoned the Penzance station and called an ambulance.'

During his years there, Derek Chappell was in a unique position to view the habits, daily life and character of those uncompromising people in Sennen Cove, and was sufficiently accepted to be able to stay around when the the mullet were being caught.

'It was quite a scene. A bustle of men, maybe forty or fifty, pulling and heaving this great mass of silver. No sightseers were tolerated and women weren't allowed anywhere near – cold iron they called them, which is Cornish for bad luck.

'Sometimes if a woman was rowing with a fisherman, she would threaten to touch his ropes – very unlucky. Women also knew they must never wave to fishermen putting out to sea. If they men saw a clergyman or a nun in the harbour they would refuse to sail, and you must never whistle or mention rabbits or pasties at sea.

'When I once went to sea out of Mousehole with some visitors and we were heading towards Lamorna, one of them pointed to the shore and said, "Look at all those rabbits over there." The boat came straight back. Cold iron, you see.'

But unquestionably the most bizarre incident in the entire career of Police Constable Derek Chappell occurred in the late sixties, which led to suggestions of international espionage and a great deal of official secrecy.

'It all started one Sunday morning when two boys turned up at the police house shaking with fear. They told me they had found a skeleton and I asked them to take me straight to the spot. We arrived at a big cliff between Land's End and Porthcurno, but the two boys wouldn't go any closer, just pointed downwards. I descended to a little cleft in the rock, and there he was. He was sitting down, and all the flesh on his hands and part of his face had gone. His feet had disintegrated too, but the rest of him was deeply tanned where the skin was showing. The pathologist told me later that he had been there three or four months and the salt action of the prevailing wind had tanned him all the way down to the bone. Rats had eaten part of him. He was dressed in a pin-striped suit.

'I marked the place with a flag and went for help. Our enquiries established that he was an American naval commander and he had been staying in a Penzance hotel. The cause of death was an overdose of drugs. I was put in a harness, and lowered over the cliff where he died and I collected phials and other stuff he had obviously dropped down.

'By then signals were flying to and from America – very interesting they were, too – and the CIA arrived along with MI5. We were instructed to forget everything we had seen or done, and no argument. Just deal with the cause of death and nothing else.

'We gathered he was being chased by agents but we never learned the real story behind it.

'The body was held in the mortuary at St Just for six months while all the fuss was going on. And because I was the Coroner's officer, I had to visit him every day, pull open his drawer and make sure nothing had been tampered with. I used to bid him "Good Morning!"

'When the body was released it was arranged for him to be cremated and his ashes sent back to his relatives in Chattanooga. I met the American Airlines stewardess who came to collect him and together we went to the funeral service. The Reverend said he was sorry about our bereavement, so we pointed out that neither of us had known him. Then the three of us went through the service, singing hymns and listening to readings. All very odd.

'A while later I got a letter from his father and mother, asking me to accept his gold pen and pencil and his American naval tie. I requested official guidance, and they said I could keep them on condition that I was not to communicate with his family in any way, shape or form. I still don't know what he was up to, but I reckon it was something to do with espionage.'

Derek Chappell, now retired to his bungalow overlooking Mount's Bay, Penzance, still has those mementoes. They are a chilling reminder of a remarkable and still unexplained incident when a solitary Cornish copper, by sheer chance, briefly encountered the mysterious world of international secret Intelligence.

8

'Voices, Voices . . . I Heard Voices'

'The dark, the serpent-haunted sea', wrote James Elroy Flecker, and it expresses poetically the belief often held by men who have spent their working lives at sea that there are strange elements at work when the tides run powerfully against them, and they begin to fear they are about to die.

John Stevens, the man who believed voices urged him to give back his life jacket when the St Ives lifeboat was about to launch to a terrible disaster in 1939, almost certainly owed his life to the intervention of 'my angels'. A fine and deeply religious man, he declared he had heard them speak to him before.

'Yes, at sea you hear 'em. Oh yes, I've been in the wheelhouse with my two knees knocking together, afraid to turn the boat round because of the sea. That's when you expose your boat, broadside to the weather, the worst position you can be in. But there comes a feeling that there is someone looking out for you.

'I recall one occasion when I was steaming through the night when I saw a single green light in front of me. Now ships over 1,600 tons have by law to carry two mast headlights, one at least ten feet higher than the other, as well as sidelights so you can tell which way the boat is sailing. But there was just one green light. How can you know what to do in circumstances like that?

'Then the voice spoke. "Port," it said. "Port your helm!" As clear as can be.

'So I did. If I hadn't, I would have collided with a big sailing ship.'

Another St Ives man had a similar uncanny experience, which had even more dramatic consequences. Eric Kemp is the only child of a well-known Cornish sea captain who spent a lifetime adventuring around the globe, from the North Atlantic to the South China seas, often away from his wife and son for two years at a time. And the son, too, could not deny the call of the sea, spending his childhood around St Ives harbour, sculling tourists to and from the pleasure boats, and when the time came demanding the chance to follow the father he scarcely knew. Eric vividly recalls the moment.

'He called me an idiot, then said he would pay for a naval education if I made a solemn promise – that I would stay at sea and not give up until I had got my Master's Certificate. I took that very seriously indeed.'

The son followed the traditional route, running regularly to India and through the Persian Gulf to Africa, trading along the coast of 'The White Man's Grave' and steadily rising through the ranks as a merchant seaman. But meeting and marrying a St Ives girl and starting a family gave him pause for thought – would he, too, become a stranger to his infant son? So he came home and joined Trinity House, eventually securing a position as second officer of their Penzance-based boat, which meant he could go home most weekends.

'Father was very upset when I left deep-sea sailing, saying I had reduced myself to a ferryboatman. But then the master's job came up on *The Queen of the Isles*, sailing from Penzance to the Scillies, and I applied and got it. So, in the end, he was satisfied. I had kept my promise.'

And in 1972, by which time he was a pilot in Penzance, Eric Kemp was invited to become the honorary secretary of the St Ives lifeboat. Within eight months he was at the centre of an incident which defies logical explanation.

'It was the beginning of August, when you get the first of the southwest gales, and a time when the boat is usually required. If you go back in the records, we always had a launch around about 3 or 4 August. There have been more rescues around that time, when the weather pattern traditionally changes, than practically any other period of the year.

'That particular day, 4 August, was sunny – but a southwest force seven was blowing outside the bay, which itself was deceptively calm. Normally lifeboatmen disappear into the community until called, but every time I turned around that day I bumped into a crew member. They pestered me to death. And from the regulars to the young hopefuls, they were all telling me there would be a launch that day. I had no such feeling and told them they were talking nonsense. But sure enough when I went home in the evening for my tea I had a call from the coastguard saying there was a little job for me. A rubber boat with a man and a small child aboard had been swept away from Porthminster Beach towards St Ives Head and would be reaching rough water and certain disaster within ten minutes. It was routine – a quick job for the inflatable inshore boat, which duly went out and grabbed it in time. It seems the man was down from Birmingham and had planned to do some fishing. When he was brought back I gave him a public dressing down for his stupidity, hoping that the lesson would sink in not only with him but with the other visitors listening. I told him that it was not a boating lake out there but a real Atlantic Ocean, next stop America 3,000 miles away!

'So after that all the lifeboatmen announced with much satisfaction: "That's it! We've had our launch for the day, we can all go home and forget about it now." But for no apparent reason a little thought in me said, "Oh no – today you're going to have a big boat launch." I confided this feeling to the cox, Tommy Cocking [grandson of Tommy Cocking who drowned in the 1939 disaster], who proceeded to give me a real lecture. He said he was taking his wife out for a Chinese meal that night; it was a special occasion, he had paid for a babysitter, and he didn't want to know.

'So I went back home but remained in a very uneasy mood. At about twenty past eight the telephone rang. It was one of the local fisherman who said he was a bit worried because one of his mates was fishing fifteen miles northeast of the Head and had been due back at 6 p.m., more than two hours ago. I told him I would have a word with the coastguards to see if anyone had heard of him or seen what he was doing. I rang the Coastguard Control at Cape Cornwall to be told they were in the middle of a long-distance medical service south of the Lizard. The man was telling me not to pester him at a time like that when it happened.

'A voice said to me: "Launch the lifeboat!"

'I blinked, looked around, but there was nobody else nearby. The coastguard was still talking away, so I told him to put the phone down because I was going to launch the lifeboat immediately. He asked me if I had gone mad, but put it down. I knew the cox wasn't around so I phoned the mechanic but he didn't answer. So I called the second cox – no answer again. But the second mechanic, Lionel Smith, was in and I told him to launch – quickly! Now Lionel, known as Lilo, is one of those unflappable people no lifeboat station should be without and he told me to calm down because I was agitated and shouting, "Get those maroons off!" I then got the tractor driver on the way down, jumped on my scooter and shot off to the lifeboat house at great speed, looking and sounding like an idiot, calling for the doors to be opened. Then Tommy Cocking arrived, swearing like a trooper, saying that there was nothing wrong with the overdue fishing boat. The lifeboat was halfway out of the boathouse at the time, and he took a very dim view of that. All the time I was demanding that the boat be launched. The other crewmen arrived and every one of them looked at me as though I had taken leave of my senses.

'Suddenly, as all this was going on, a red flare went arcing up over the bay. It came from a brand-new ketch which had sailed from the Scillies, got into trouble with her steering and was heading helplessly in the southwest gale for the shore on the other side of the bay.

'Everything was in place and moving. Instead of taking fifteen minutes, within six minutes or less the lifeboat was launched and on its way across the bay. The men got to the ketch just as it reached the surf close to a rock, didn't have time to put anyone on board, but managed to get a rope over and haul it out of trouble. There were four adults and three children aged around six or seven aboard her – beautiful, blue-eyed kids with blond hair. If that boat had gone either on to the rocks or the beach in those conditions I wouldn't have given those kids any chance at all.

'When the children eventually arrived on the quay and looked at me, the whole point of being in a lifeboat society, all the rushing around and all the organising, it all seemed worthwhile. I put their photograph, taken as they landed, up on the boathouse wall. I don't think I had a higher moment than that during eleven years of uproar every week as the honorary secretary. I had a marvellous time with the St Ives lifeboat, but everything is in that picture.

'I cannot explain my behaviour, but I thought I heard a voice. It clearly said I must launch the lifeboat now, and I turned round to see where it had come from. I am a Christian and believe that God speaks through the Bible, but when I hear of people saying that God has spoken to them I become very sceptical.

'But there I was, gibbering like an idiot. All I could do was scream at everyone to launch the lifeboat. They had every reason to believe I had snapped, but then that red flare went up . . .'

Yet another mysterious incident happened as recently as 1989, far away from Cornwall – an ocean apart, in fact. On 1 November 1889, there was a lifeboat tragedy near the Giant's Causeway off the coast of Northern Ireland. The Portrush boat went to the aid of a sailing ship in distress. The ship got away safely but the lifeboat was driven ashore and three crewmen died. Exactly 100 years later on 1 November 1989, the honorary secretary of the Portrush lifeboat, John Scott, a crew member himself in previous years, organised a commemoration. He tells the story of what happened in a very deliberate, almost faraway manner, as if he is still trying to work it out.

'I had a large square wreath made out of paper flowers so that it would float. We launched with the Chairman of the Branch, the crew and members of the Coastguard since one of the men who died had also been a coastguard. It was a bad old day, but we arrived at the spot where it happened at ten o'clock in the morning, which was exactly the time of the disaster a century before.

'The wreath was duly placed in the sea. Then a very odd thing occurred. It didn't move. There was a big sea running but the wreath seemed to be anchored there. I would have expected it to have been swept away immediately. And when the lifeboat steamed off a little later it still stayed put. It remained there for as long as we could see it.

'Now lifeboat crews are not normally very religious, but that made our men wonder . . .'

9

The Captain and the Storm Petrel

When Captain Eric Kemp relinquished his position with the St Ives lifeboat, he handed over to another master mariner, Captain Dennis Proudfoot, who eventually passed the baton to yet another master mariner, Captain Philip Moran, the current honorary secretary. Now if you study the RNLI handbook, which lists the officers of each of the 273 stations around the coasts of Britain and Ireland, you will notice that many of the honorary secretaries bear the title of captain, indicating a history of long and distinguished service at sea, necessary for the vital duties of the office since the honorary secretary is in command until the lifeboat is launched.

Most, if not all of them, can spin fascinating yarns of hair-raising experiences at sea, but probably none is more varied or exciting than the life and career of Captain Philip Moran. And the later years of that career are shrouded in mystery and intrigue.

A very tall and lean figure, with hair nowadays bleached white and a face deeply etched by his years 'before the mast', drama entered his life when he just a child. Born in St Ives in 1936, he – like Eric Kemp – lacked the presence and influence of a father as he grew up. But he was not the son of a seaman. His father was a captain, yes, but in the Indian Army. When war broke out in 1939, the army required the family to move to Plymouth where they were bombed out of their home. They sought sanctuary on a farm near Newton Abbot in Devon but life was disrupted again when the Allied armies massed along the south coast to prepare for the Normandy landings, and needed the farm. Philip's mother stayed on to do the catering for the troops, but he and his two brothers and two sisters were not allowed to stay. Nor were they were granted the privilege of remaining together, so Philip found himself at the age of seven travelling on a train with twenty other evacuees, all strangers.

'My brothers and sisters were sent off all around the place, but by an odd quirk of fate I fetched up in St Ives. But my home town was also on a total war footing, full of British commandos and American Marines training for the invasion, and none of my relatives could take me in because they had no room – they were boarding soldiers like most other people.

'Anyway the twenty-one children were put into the back of a truck and taken round to a list of people who said they were prepared to take in an evacuee. But there were only twenty names on the list. So when they ran out of households there was bound to be one left.

'It turned out to be me. Alone and unwanted. I think it damaged my confidence for years – that, and being ultra-thin. Anyway, someone had a brainwave and they took me to see a lady called Mrs Farnham, who lived right on Porthmeor Beach. She already had thirteen children in her care and when she was asked if she would look after me she said that one more wouldn't make any difference, so I moved in. I stayed there for two years and it was a happy time.

'Mrs Farnham believed we should all stick together, which created a problem on the religious front. There was a lot of pressure on her to send us to the various churches to which the evacuees were attached, so she settled for us all working through the entire spectrum of religion in St Ives. One day we would go, say, to the Parish church in the morning, the Catholic church in the afternoon and one of the Methodist chapels in the evening. The next week we would go to a Plymouth Brethren service, and so on.

'The point of removing us from a place of danger to St Ives was almost made nonsense one morning when we were all on Porthmeor Beach having a sandcastle competition. Suddenly a plane came swooping up over the island which rises at the end of the beach and we started waving to it. Then it began machine-gunning the sand. It also dropped one bomb on the nearby gasworks and another on a couple of houses a little further away, by which time we were all under the big table in the kitchen.

'One day someone came to say that my mother was moving back to St Ives and would come to claim me. They tell me I would get up every morning for two weeks and sit in a corner of the garden, waiting for her to come and claim me. But it was two months before she appeared. However, I didn't lose faith – I just kept waiting.

'The first time I recall seeing my father was when I was twelve. At the time I was home on holiday from a military college. Mother told me that he was upstairs, and not feeling very well. So I went up, and there was this very thin and very brown man lying in bed. He had to come back to Britain when India was given independence and he hated St Ives. Over there, even an ordinary white person led a very good life with servants and all the trimmings. He had enjoyed a particularly good deal, and hadn't wanted to leave.

'He only stayed with us for a few weeks, and then went to live with his brother in Surrey.'

Philip Moran's status as the son of an army officer gave him entry to the Duke of York's Military College at Dover during the war. Apparently the discipline was severe but fair, and Philip declares it gave him 'a bit of backbone'.

'But when I was about fifteen I decided I didn't want to go into the army, and very quietly looked into the possibility of going to Hendon Police College. I wanted to be a detective. Unfortunately I was a bit naïve, and after receiving my application in writing the police college naturally wrote to the military college for a reference. I was marched in front of the Commandant who told me in no uncertain terms that if I had no desire to pursue a career in the army, then I would have to leave at the end of the summer term.

'So I ended back in St Ives, much to my father's displeasure, and took a job with a gentlemen's outfitter. One day I was up a ladder cleaning his windows when an old school friend came to chat and told me he had secured a place at a navigation school in Plymouth and was going to be a sea captain. It sounded better than the job I was doing, so I asked him how to apply, got a day off from my job, and went along for an interview. That was on a Thursday. I was rather startled to be told that I could start the following Monday. On Tuesday I was sent to be measured for a naval uniform and arrived home on the Saturday resplendent in my new outfit, all aglow with midshipman's gold. Mother was delighted. My sister took me to my first dance at The Guildhall that night to show me off. I was fifteen, very thin, six feet two inches in height, and very shy.

'Just inside The Guildhall there were two or three rows of seats traditionally occupied by older women, aged around thirty, who hadn't yet managed to find a husband. They used to make acidic comments about the people entering the dance. What happened next I will not forget to my dying day. One of those ladies, whose nickname was Mary Mouth, took one look at me in my uniform, which still had to experience any salt water around it, and shouted: "Last week he was a tailor's apprentice, and this week he's an admiral!"

'I turned around, walked straight out of The Guildhall, and I never wore my uniform in St Ives again.'

Now most seamen who aspire to the senior ranks have been wedded to the sea since childhood, accustomed to helping out in the harbour, working the skiffs, handling ropes, anchors, mizzen masts and generally learning basic seacraft. Not so Captain Philip Moran.

'Yes, that is something which has plagued me throughout my life because people assume I must have always had a great love for the sea. This was definitely not the case. I didn't have a clue about the sea when I was accepted at the Navigation College in Plymouth. I'd never been on a boat, not even a rowing boat. I had no particular yearning for the sea. The only reason I applied for the college was that becoming a captain seemed like a good idea, and – more importantly – I had to do something more ambitious than working in a gentlemen's outfitters. I wanted to climb the ladder as far as possible and help provide a better life for my mother, who was not having an easy time.

'When I graduated and joined a shipping line my first experience at sea was terrible. We sailed out of Glasgow on passage to Panama and ran straight into a force nine southwesterly gale. I had never been so violently ill in my life. But I was not allowed to stay in bed. I had to stand, as a cadet, in the wing of the bridge and no excuses accepted. I felt very much like dying, and if I could have got off the ship that day I would never have gone near the sea again. Even when I came off watch I was only in bed for two hours when they hauled me back on deck to solve a flooding problem. I was hung by my ankles over the side to clear some blocked scupper pipes which they couldn't reach from on deck.

'But the officers on that ship were applying a system which worked. By teatime the following day I was so ravenously hungry that I had forgotten about seasickness. And that was it. One night of horror, and I was never seasick again.'

For the next twenty years, Philip Moran adventured around the world, once caught in the middle of Fidel Castro's revolution in Cuba, stranded in Trinidad for three months, on the fringe of conflict once again, in the Middle East in Cyprus, working out of New York on a luxury liner . . . and sending money back home to his mother.

He rose through the ranks to first officer, passed all the examinations and qualified as a master mariner at the age of twenty-six. Having the ticket is one thing, but securing your own ship to command was quite another in the British Merchant Navy. Even when there were 3,000 ships sailing under the red duster it was very rare for a master mariner to be handed a captaincy before his late thirties, and by the time Phillip joined the queue the British merchant fleet was in decline.

But as hundreds of his shipmates were made redundant, he was retained, and sent to Cornwall to look after a small fleet of unwanted vessels anchored in tiers on the River Fal. When that job finished, he was offered a position on a refrigerated meat ship trading to Argentina. Fortunately – as it turned out – he refused to take it.

'I was in my mid-thirties, I had worked hard, obeyed the rules and been given very little chance of a social life. A first officer only had a couple of weeks off a year. I wanted to go back home to St Ives, sit on the beach and contemplate life. It so happened that the ship I would have been on had I taken the job was hit by a tanker, turned into a fireball and everyone was killed.

'It was fate . . . luck.

'St Ives is a timeless place, a place you can come back to and no one would realise you had been away for years. People just thought they hadn't seen you for a while. All my family had left by then, but I knew it was a place where I could re-establish myself within minutes. I had some money saved, it was the beginning of the 1970s and life was wonderful. I was unmarried, the social and sexual revolution was under way with the advent of the pill, I had the beads around my neck and went to the beach every day listening to Dylan and the Moody Blues. I had a sense of social stability at last, moved into a house with a group of other people and did no work.

'It was coming on for the second winter when the money ran out. But I had a wonderful bank manager, quite an old man, and he gave me an overdraft of £3,000, which was a lot of money in those days.

He said he wasn't worried because I had the qualifications and when the time was right he knew I would go back to my career. Eventually his money disappeared, too, and one day as I was walking down to the beach I tripped on some steps and ripped a heel off my shoe. And the realisation dawned – I couldn't even afford to have it mended. When I arrived at the beach I announced that I needed to get a job. Someone had a newspaper and they noticed that a government organisation was offering a job requiring my qualifications.

'I was invited for an interview in Wales. I took out an old suit which I think had belonged to my father, found some shoes which were too small for me, and caught a train to Bristol where I stayed overnight with a friend. I was thirty-eight, had no home, two shillings and sixpence in my pocket and a £3,000 overdraft.

'I had a hangover in the morning, caught the wrong train, and arrived for the interview about four hours late. They were still waiting for me. The money was not good, the position was an inferior one and the organisation itself sounded very vague. So when they offered me the job I turned it down. They then declared they wouldn't take no for an answer and told me to go home and think about it.

'So I did – and bumped into the bank manager. He knew I had gone after a job and when I told him I had refused it he was horrified at first and then philosophical about it. I sat on the beach again – thought – and came to the conclusion that I owed that man. So when they wrote to me at the end of the week and offered me the job again, I accepted.'

By so doing, Philip Moran launched into a phase of his career which frequently defies description and, indeed, to a certain extent must deny the telling on the grounds of national security. At first he had no idea of the curious, secretive world he was entering. He was put into a four-star hotel, everything on the bill, sent home after only four days on a lavish allowance, and promoted! Totally bewildered, he later met a fellow officer whom he had worked with in the merchant navy and asked him if he knew what on earth was going on. He was advised not to ask questions, just to enjoy it.

In fact, he had been signed up by a government research organisation and was eventually obliged to sign a pledge of confidentiality under the Official Secrets Act. The skill and experience that his new masters had obviously discovered even before that curious interview led him to various periods of command, and a series of missions over the next twelve years which ranged from the hilarious to the downright dangerous.

But one incident which remains most vividly in his mind brought him up against hazards created entirely by Nature, not man. He was in command of a research vessel which was regarded as one of the world's finest, and, with its equipment, worth a breathtakingly large sum. It all began when he was ordered to enter the Antarctic for a one-month research cruise. But the ship was delayed in Brazil and instead of going in during the benevolent summer he navigated in a month late when all the other research vessels had pulled out.

'I ran into a seventy- to eighty-mile-an-hour gale, and had to heave to for four days because of the violence of the weather. The full force of the southern ocean was coming at us with no barriers or shelter. The waves measured up to eighty feet. We had to nurse the ship the entire time, manoeuvring to get it up each wave and then cutting the power off to get it down the other side. I had an officer steering, another on the engine controls and I was standing against the wheelhouse window shouting out orders.

'I had no sleep for four days and nights. I must have smoked hundreds of cigarettes and drunk innumerable cups of coffee. There came a moment two or three days into it when I recall standing at the window thinking I couldn't cope any more. I just wanted to hand over the whole bloody business to someone else. But I was the captain and I was stuck there.

'Just then I saw a petrel flying past the bridge. The wind must have been blowing seventy miles an hour and there was this tiny, tiny bird going about its business as if the gale were all in a day's work. So, I thought that if that small bundle of skin and feathers can handle this with no signs of distress then so could I. It spurred me on.

'At 5 a.m. on the fourth day the wind dropped. It was a wonderful feeling. I stayed on watch another couple of hours to make sure, before going down to my cabin to rest. I thought I would sleep for days, but I was awake after two hours. So I decided to order work to start and we got the scientific gear into the water. Then I signed the night orders and went to bed at 11.30 p.m. At two in the morning I was called to the bridge. The gale had returned in full force.

'We were back in an even worse mess with 8,000 metres of wire loaded with instruments trailing behind the ship. Slowly, slowly we eased her down, trying to balance keeping her up to the wind and the sea and at the same time avoiding dropping back on to the wire as we pulled it in. If it had got around the propeller that would have been the end of it. We would have been helpless. We had a chap in charge of the wire and made sure he had these huge wire cutters. I had a word with him and said that if I gave the order he must cut the lot away, and to hell with the expense. The equipment was worth hundreds of thousands, never mind the boat – and that cost millions. Eventually we hauled it all back in without incident.

'Then I realised that if it got any worse we would be facing another four days unable to move. So I decided to try a very risky way out. I turned her round in the waves to put the wind and sea to the stern so we could run with it. If you are caught on the quarter doing this manoeuvre it corkscrews the ship, which means you roll and pitch at the same time. I gave her everything on the engines and went for it. For the first twenty minutes we got away with it but suddenly she was caught, and corkscrewed. Everything went, things began smashing up and down throughout the ship, a very dangerous situation. I pressed on, but resolved to heave to and sit it out if that happened again.

'But it didn't. We ran like a bird – like that petrel – for forty-eight hours and eventually made it to Capetown.'

Philip Moran, who never married, relinquished his position with the government agency at the age of forty-nine, negotiated a handsome settlement and returned to St Ives. He had made the bank manager a happy man again long before. Today, he lives contentedly in a fully paid for cottage which overlooks the harbour in St Ives, and is less than thirty paces from the lifeboat house.

Naturally, such close proximity allied to his qualifications led to an offer of a place in the management team of the St Ives lifeboat. In 1989, he became their deputy launching authority and the following year moved into the senior position.

His first lifeboat experience, however, was on the receiving end when he suffered what at first appeared to be a heart attack whilst on his research ship in the middle of a storm off the Hebrides – Philip's career highlights seem to be mostly set against a background of violent weather.

The Oban lifeboat arrived to take him to hospital, but Philip refused to be transferred on a stretcher.

'Although I was suffering from severe chest pains, I wasn't happy at the prospect of being lowered over the ship's side wrapped in a stretcher in those conditions so I insisted on climbing down a ladder. I spent five days in intensive care. Then the doctors discovered I had some kind of chest virus, which I was most pleased to hear.'

Philip Moran has been at the centre of a succession of notable incidents since he began his RNLI service, for St Ives is a busy station. One of the more curious demonstrated the risks that people are prepared to take when their pets are in peril.

'The chain of events was quite odd. It was a late-night call, which started when the coastguards rang me to say they had been telephoned by a gentleman who thought he had heard a call for help whilst walking along Porthmeor Beach. But they weren't too sure how valid the information was because the gentleman sounded as if he had been drinking. However, our policy is to go even if a hoax is suspected so I ordered the launch of the inshore boat. They searched one end of the bay without finding anything, then moved to the other side as the tide began to ebb away strongly – and came across a man clinging to a small oil drum. He was fully clothed, semi-conscious and just beginning to go into the main tide. Any later and he would have just disappeared.

'He was in an extreme state of hypothermia, so the crew called me on the way back to send for an ambulance. Unfortunately, the ambulance broke down and the replacement became delayed. So we had to administer first aid ourselves in the boathouse – lifeboat crews are trained for this. We put him in a special body bag to warm him up and by the time an ambulance finally arrived he was fully conscious and had managed to drink a cup of tea. He was very grateful, and as he came to he asked a rather surprising question: "Has anyone seen my dog?"

'It seems his dog had gone into the sea on Porthmeor, been swept away and he plunged in to rescue it. Of course, he had been caught by the ebb, too. That was one very fortunate man. First of all, an oil drum just happened to float by him. Then his shouts were heard by just one person, who had, as it happened, been imbibing and wasn't too sure about the situation. But he mentioned it to his wife when he arrived home and it was she who insisted he telephoned the coastguards.

'As the dog owner went off to spend a night in hospital we discussed the question of the missing dog with the police, who very obligingly went out into the night to look for it. They eventually found the dog sitting on a rock under a cliff close to where his master had been picked up.

'The two were reunited the following day. And a very pleasing moment that was.'

There was another drama involving a person being swept into the sea which again had a happy ending but led to a high level of frustration for the lifeboatmen of St Ives – and once again underlines how responsibly they treat any information, however dubious.

It began under Philip Moran's nose, so to speak. The balcony of his cottage juts out over a walkway alongside a beach which is regularly pounded by heavy seas, particularly during spring tides. Waves can burst clean over Philip's roof. A group of boys were playing a game of dare, dodging the waves, when one – dressed in a wet suit – was carried away. The lifeboat was being launched when the boy's father, who wasn't far away, was informed. Bravely, he immediately dived into the sea, swam to his son and hauled him safely to the shore. But that wasn't the end of the matter, as Philip ruefully recalls.

'We were preparing to wind down the search operation after hearing that the boy was safe when a very distraught woman ran into the boathouse and said she had seen another boy go into the water. The information she offered was very sparse and no one else had reported it, but she was very insistent. Now at times of crisis like that people can suffer shock of varying degrees. Sometimes they see things which may be real, or may be imaginary.

'But she felt so strongly about it that we decided to continue looking. The whole area was floodlit by the coastguards, and we started a very elaborate search pattern which involved both lifeboats, a helicopter and the police. As this was going on, we tracked down the other boys who had been on the walkway. They had run home in a panic. They, in turn, identified other children around at the time and they were located, too. We also called the woman back to the boathouse and asked if she could remember what the boy had been wearing. She described a wet suit with roughly the same colours worn by the rescued boy.

'Eventually, we established beyond doubt that the second boy she thought she had seen fall in was, in fact, the one saved by his father. But it took well over two hours before we were satisfied that all possibilities had been eliminated and the full search pattern completed. That is the job of the RNLI.'

Philip Moran found himself embarrassingly on the other side of a lifeboat service for a second time when he sailed out to do some sport fishing with a couple of friends, and the engine of his boat broke down about ten miles down the coast towards Land's End.

'It was Sunday lunchtime and a beautiful day with a flat calm sea. At the time I was the deputy launching authority. I radioed the coastguards to tell them about the problem, stressing that I was in no danger, but if they would kindly contact any passing fishing boats, I would appeciate a tow back to St Ives.

'It appears they couldn't locate any in my area so, in their wisdom, launched the lifeboat! It caused a great deal of hilarity, and led to several very public notices displayed in local pubs describing how the very brave lifeboatmen had left their lunchtime pints untouched to respond to this rescue call.

'And as they told me when putting the towline aboard, they had been led to believe I had a semi-nude woman on the boat and that was the only reason they had turned out!'

10

Brush with Danger

Amid the pantheon of classic hero figures, the lifeboat coxswain has a special place in the esteem of the public. An image has been fashioned down the generations, led by those mesmerising Victorian and Edwardian studio portraits of medal-winning coxes of the past, sou'wester framing granite-hewn features, muscular frame bulging out of a cork life jacket, hands turned to iron by years of wrestling with storm-racked ships' wheels.

Real men . . . mighty men. The thought of their being engaged in any activity less than physically challenging cannot be entertained. You would not expect a lifeboat cox to be, say, a butterfly collector, a dress designer, a Morris dancer. Or an artist . . .

Yet there are two very distinguished coxes, one retired and one very much active, who between them can display two silver medals, three bronze and a BEM (plus an appearance on *This Is Your Life*, an institution which seems very partial to coxes), and who have, in fact, firmly established themselves as artists, and not by any means amateurs occasionally sloshing around on a canvas at weekends. These men are serious artists, recognised by their peers, and are receiving serious money for their work. Up to £1,000, in one case.

The senior of this unusual pair is Derek Scott, who freely admits that he makes a good living from his paintings, which appear to be exclusively studies of lifeboat dramas. He says he committed to memory his most dangerous moments on the lifeboat, preparatory to placing them on canvas. A brush with danger in every sense. He has a wealth of such moments stored away, because he became the cox of the Mumbles lifeboat in South Wales at the age of twenty-six, then the youngest ever appointed by the RNLI. He has two silver medals, one bronze, the BEM and the famous Red Book.

The second is Eric Ward, statuesque cox of the St Ives lifeboat in Cornwall, who has two bronze medals and some way to go. He dominates the harbour in St Ives rather like that large fellow who once towered over the harbour on the Greek island of Rhodes, with one foot on one side and the second on the other. There is an uncanny echo with Eric Ward, who is over six feet five inches in his sea boots. In addition to his lifeboat responsibilities, he is also the harbour master, with an office on one side of St Ives harbour. The lifeboat house (a superb new structure) is on the other. Eric is an unmissable sight as he strides between his two command posts.

When he dons his artist's hat he specialises in nudes, seascapes and interiors, and in 1994 had a very successful one-man exhibition with an abundance of red dots, signifying sold paintings. Thirty canvases went through the door, one priced at £800. His work has also sold in Bristol, London, Plymouth and Antwerp, and he is a member of the Chelsea Arts Club.

At first, neither man seemed destined for a senior lifeboat career. Eric's mother wanted him to be a teacher, he wanted to be a fisherman. He trained to be a teacher but didn't follow through and ended up as a policeman (no problems with height, of course). He administered law and order in Cardiff and Penzance before realising his early ambition and returning home to be a St Ives fisherman. As a youngster he had spent his spare time on local boats. But he did have a tragic family background. His father died when he was nine, his mother six years later, and parental duties were assumed by his elder sister.

It was Eric's mother who ignited the interest in art. St Ives, of course, has long been a haven for artists and as a kid he would be given half a crown (12.5p) by her to go to Leonard Fuller's art classes on Saturday mornings – more to get rid of him than anything else, he claims.

As for Derek Scott, he declares that as a boy, art was the only thing that he was ever good at or interested in. His parents recognised this and encouraged him at the age of fourteen to sit the examination for Swansea Art College. He not only passed, but became one of the only two art students in the whole of Wales to be given a grant that year. He stayed there until he reached eighteen in 1946, which meant he was due for National Service. His father, who had risen swiftly to the rank of commander in the Royal Naval Volunteer Reserve because of his engineering skill, drilled the young man into how to go about persuading the recruitment board to find him a place in the navy. Derek had other ideas.

'By that time I'd had the navy up to my ears. I was a bit of a rebel teenager, stupid really, and I applied to join the army. When I came home and told my father, he was absolutely taken aback, and then said I would have to learn my lesson the hard way, as he had done. You see, he volunteered at sixteen to serve in the army in 1914 when the First World War began. He was sent to the front, and managed to survive the entire war. Not many did that. When he was demobbed he swore that he would never go back in the trenches if it happened again, and joined the RNVR.

'He was in the thick of it again during the Second World War, serving in a very fast small boat delivering and picking up spies in and out of German-occupied Europe. He told me about one amazing occasion when he and his crew went to pick up some people coming out of a designated part of the French coast. They were instructed not to wait if their passengers hadn't turned up by a certain time. But being soft-hearted they waited another five minutes, and that was their undoing. They went aground on the beach, unable to move. My father said it was the longest night of his life, waiting for dawn to break and the tide to rise. When the water did come around the boat, they jumped out and shoved it across the mud. By the time they were spotted they were going like hell. And the people never did turn up. He did several trips like that.

'A lot of my own military service was spent on the border between Italy and Yugoslavia where there was the occasional spot of bother, but I didn't see action like my father.

'When I was demobbed he wanted me to go back to the art college for another three years to become properly qualified. I resisted – student life had ceased to appeal – so he said in that case I had better go into business with him. He was converting and building boats, so I became a shipwright and stayed with him until my mid-twenties.'

This flight from the schoolroom in search of action was to be repeated a generation later by Eric Ward. Dutifully following his late mother's wishes, he won a place at teacher training college.

He confesses he never wanted to teach, considered it would be a boring occupation and at the end of the course just packed up and came home to St Ives without a Teacher's Certificate.

Both men had been drawn to the sea from infancy, learned basic seamanship in small boats and from helping fishermen, and became involved in the lifeboat service as young men. In the case of Derek Scott, it was against a background of tragedy.

'I came out of the army in June 1947 and joined immediately – because the Mumbles lifeboat didn't have a crew. They were all lost on the night of 23 April, just a few days before my return, when a hurricane struck our bay and a coaster called the *San Tampa* was washed ashore at Porthcawl.

'One of the old boys told me that the swell was so great that night that our lifeboat, the *Edward Prince of Wales*, was afloat on its chocks before they could get it out of the door – and the lifeboat house is eighty feet above sea level. They left at dusk, but had to return to get an update of the *San Tampa*'s position. There was no radio in those days. They set off again and that was the last anyone saw them alive. Their boat was found upside down not far from the coaster, with the bodies some distance away which clearly indicated they had suffered a capsize. Eight of them, and they had all been choked by fuel oil from the *San Tampa*, which had snapped in two. Their kapok life jackets had absorbed the oil which turned them into anchors around their necks, dragging their heads under the water. And they were all absolutely black. You couldn't recognise them. A team of men went over and washed them all in paraffin before they were buried in the local cemetery. Terrible.

'That lifeboat had been obliged to run across a series of sandbanks and go to a lee shore without any lights. I only ever worked once in a true hurricane, and that was in deep water, so I know from experience that trying to manoeuvre in shallow water must have been virtually impossible.

'I imagine that the cox, Billy Gammon, must have known the odds were great but he had succeeded in a similar situation not long before when another ship went aground in the same area. He had managed to get all the crew safely off that time by dropping an anchor and going on to the casualty using a drogue to give stability. He was obviously hoping to pull off the same trick twice.

'But that was a night like no other. The sea rose to a height it had never reached before. The *San Tampa* had been swept away on the rocks on the edge of a golf course, which was so flooded that they had no idea where the water's edge was. There was no sophisticated equipment to assist them, just lead and line. Just to give you some idea of the force of the elements, the anchor chain of the lifeboat had split the stem post straight down.

'Years later when I was cox, I had to use the same technique on the same beach where those lads had drowned. I was facing up to the situation that Billy Gammon came up against, except that it wasn't blowing a hurricane. Not far short, though – gale force ten. It was a very, very eerie feeling.

'A big floating crane, capable of lifting a hundred tons, had broken loose with the whole crew aboard and we were trying to get them off. The damn thing was towering eighty feet above us, and I was scared that it would topple over and smash us to pieces. I dropped the anchor and ran the cable out. We were well offshore, to make sure that as long as that anchor held we had a good chance of hauling ourselves out of trouble. I was also using the drogue which is like a canvas ice-cream cone, three feet across, with a small outlet at the narrow end. You tow it fat end first and the lifeboat becomes like a spider hanging on to a strong web. It's very useful but when you are doing the manoeuvre I was engaged in that time, there comes a point when you let the anchor go and you must get the drogue back in. It becomes dangerous to leave it out.

'But as we were going in to try and take the people off the floating crane, the boat spun round and the drogue was carried past us and into the shore side. Seven men were trying to drag it in, but all the time the breaking sea was filling it even though it was back to front. At first it was more than they could manage. But they eventually retrieved it, and we got the crew safely off the floating crane.'

Before he became a cox, Derek Scott was taught navigation by his father and gained experience of big ships by working on vessels in and around the Bristol Channel. In 1955, at the tender age of twenty-six, he was earning nine pounds a week as a shipwright when an RNLI inspector arrived and offered him the full-time position as cox of the Mumbles lifeboat. The crew had voted for him.

'But I didn't want to do it. My wife, Patricia, was also opposed to the idea. For one thing, the pay was only six pounds a week. Eventually the inspector persuaded me to try it for a month to see if I was suitable. Thirty-two years later, when I retired, I still hadn't heard a thing!'

In St Ives, Eric Ward had a parallel experience, in that a high and responsible office was thrust at him. He was very happy working his fishing boat and serving on the lifeboat when in 1985 the position of harbour master in St Ives fell vacant. Like Derek Scott, he became a reluctant candidate.

'I had no wish to do the job. I enjoyed fishing and the thought of giving that up to deal with other people's problems did not appeal. But the retiring harbour master suggested I should apply, which I did although I was sure I wouldn't get the job. I was shortlisted, but still thought I had little chance. Then they offered it to me, and now I'm glad they did. It's probably the best thing I've done, and it turned out to be an interesting occupation. And as you get older, and I am over fifty now, security becomes more important.'

In 1989, when Tommy Cocking retired, the harbour master was voted in as cox, a remarkable double honour. Both his Bronze Medals were won on the inshore boat, both within the surf line, immeasurably the most perilous position to be in in a boat. Eric Kemp, the honorary secretary, whose remarkable premonition once saved an entire family, had a hand in the first one. He spotted a sailing dinghy, being handled with obvious incompetence by four teenage youths, heading out to sea in a force six onshore northerly.

'We were already halfway across the bay when they capsized going over the sand bar into the Hayle River. So we scooted into the surf and picked them up. They had no life jackets and there was a strong undertow. If Eric hadn't called the boat when he did, they would have probably drowned.

'The second one was in an even more hazardous situation. A yacht was reported aground close to Zennor. It was at the time of the Falklands War so that helicopter cover wasn't very good. We were on the spot long before the helicopter arrived. There was a self-inflating life raft against the cliff, but we found no one in it on investigation, and a yacht partially submerged nearby. There was no one in that either. A body was picked up three weeks later. He must have been asleep when the yacht ran in towards the shore and the surf was so fierce it probably sank immediately.'

Eric Ward nominates as his worst moment of his career in the lifeboat as the partial capsize on the big boat in 1977, when Tommy

Cocking was the cox. He admits that it did frighten him, but on the other hand gave him confidence in RNLI boat design. For Derek Scott, the nightmare moment (a very long moment, actually) came in 1963.

'As I was going to bed that night they were forecasting a hurricane. I listened to the short-wave radio upstairs and heard the coastguards talking about a ship called the *Kilo* on fire off the southern coast of Ireland. So I rang the coastguards to see if there was anything in the offing for me, and they said there wasn't. Because of that forecast there were no ships in my area so I thought, thank God, and went to bed more relaxed, but thinking about those poor men off the coast of Ireland. At three o'clock in the morning my telephone rang. It was the honorary secretary, Captain Mock. He said there was a ship on fire and in big trouble, and would I go out to her? So I said: "That ship is off southern Ireland."

'"Not any more," said the captain. "It's coming up the Bristol Channel!"

'I just couldn't understand that at first, but it turned out that the ship was carrying forty-gallon drums of sodium on deck. Now sodium ignites on contact with water, so you cannot imagine a worse deck cargo in a hurricane. And one of the drums had punctured, exploded and caused the rest to begin igniting one after the other. The whole damn ship was on fire.

'The Dutch skipper couldn't run for Ireland although it was a lot nearer because it would have meant sailing into the face of the storm. The bridge, steering and all accommodation were at the stern of the ship and the fire would have engulfed the entire crew, which numbered ten. His only choice was to run before the weather towards England, which meant that the flames would be blown away from the bridge. He had been doing that all night. They had launched the Tenby lifeboat, but the *Kilo* went out of its range; then the Appledore boat tried but couldn't get over the very difficult bar between them and the sea; so the Ilfracombe was considered but the idea was abandoned because it was only a small, thirty-six-foot carriage boat. Ours was a forty-seven-footer, although it was an open boat with no cabin or wheelhouse. So we were called.

'We went out to try and find the boat in a sea so enormous that we seemed to travel two steps forward, and one back. The lifeboat was standing up vertically. Then an aircraft contacted us on the radio. It was a Shackleton, with a big radar in its belly, way up above the storm, and he wanted to know what our position was. I will always remember the mechanic saying: "Bloody desperate!" Then the pilot said he had found us, came down and brought the plane low over the boat and rumbled his engines. It was a signal to follow him. What he did then was to drop parachute flares as he disappeared – and they worked just like Catseyes in the road. Next the Shackleton went to the *Kilo* and did exactly the same thing in reverse. He was aiming us together, you see.

'Then we saw the *Kilo*. At first it was as if someone had struck a match on the horizon. But he was coming at speed with the wind behind him and within no time the flames got bigger and bigger. During the war Swansea was bombed flat – and I saw it, a town on fire. And that was exactly what this ship looked like.

'As we got nearer we saw the explosions. Every now and again one of the barrels would hurtle up like fireworks in the sky, then come down to create huge pools of fire. The captain stopped his ship and we attempted to come alongside but the rise and fall of the sea was forty feet from trough to the crest, measured on the Shackleton's radar. The sea was on fire all around the ship. We then tried to get under her stern twice. The second time she rolled broadside and we very nearly ended up in his hold. We shot away under his bow and the captain then told me over his radio that he proposed to steam towards Swansea, which was the best thing he could do under the circumstances, since he didn't appear to be in danger of sinking.

'We followed him in. I could see the crew out on the deck, huddled at the back end of the ship trying to keep away from the heat. The minute the captain tucked his ship in behind Swansea Head away from the full ferocity of the weather I jammed the lifeboat right under her stern. The second cox jumped forward and attached our new nylon bow rope to the *Kilo* – nylon had just come in and that rope was the pride and joy of the vessel. As he did so, explosions started up on the ship and as he dashed back it started raining fire. We all went under the cuddy – a canopy. When it stopped all the *Kilo*'s crew rushed out and jumped on to the lifeboat, captain as well. We jammed them under the canopy for protection and I backed away, trying to part the rope because no one was going forward to pull it off. But I couldn't bust it. It was like a great piece of elastic. We had had no experience of nylon before, you see. Finally, the second cox put a hatchet through it. The *Kilo* drifted away into the bay and finally beached.

'Amazingly, as we left it there was a cloudburst so heavy you could scarcely breathe. It actually knocked the fire out. The ship survived. Later on the captain asked me to put him and the chief engineer back on board. We got the engines started and took her into Swansea harbour.

'All the upper decks had melted. Hanging over like chewing gum.'

Derek Scott was awarded the silver medal for that astonishing exploit. He put in forty years with the lifeboat service altogether, which earned him the British Empire Medal, another silver, a bronze and a surprise visit from Eamonn Andrews in 1987. And he still soldiers on for the RNLI, a prized asset like Eric Ward, who has received a lot of media attention. Derek's paintings of lifeboat rescues fetch between £350 and £1,000 – sometimes for the benefit of the RNLI. He is also in demand as a speaker, for he clearly has the Celtic gift of expressing himself poetically, and never fails to use these opportunities to proclaim the message of the lifeboat service.

11

Born to be Cox . . . and Coxswain Hornblower

If ever a man was born to be cox, then it must be Tommy Cocking, who commanded the St Ives lifeboat for twenty-two years. In the St Ives boathouse there is an antique photograph of the christening ceremony of a boat called the *Caroline Parsons*. The year is 1934, and a three-year-old boy is standing proudly among the crew – the infant Tommy Cocking. The cox? He's called Tommy Cocking, too. The boy's grandfather. On the other side of the cox is Tommy's father – yet another Thomas, a crewman. His Uncle Jack Cocking is there too, and his uncle by marriage Richard Quick Stevens. From childhood the boy in the picture had set his heart on wearing the white-topped hat that distinguishes a coxswain. He served for fifteen years on the crew before it was bestowed, and then made many sacrifices in a material sense. For it is clear that coxes were underpaid until recently. His grandfather made the ultimate sacrifice, drowned in the disaster launch of 1939.

Tommy Cocking was a cox of the old school, a fierce disciplinarian. He says he modelled himself on his grandfather, whom he clearly idolised. Many an aspiring crewman has been scorched by the anger of Tommy, if he was judged to have erred in some way. It was said that his glare could fry eggs at ten paces.

His bravery became a legend in the lifeboat service. He once declared on a network television documentary that he would never refuse to launch, whatever the conditions, if there was a casualty out there, and was as good as his word. That courage was officially recognised in 1984 when the Queen Mother presented him with the Maud Smith Award for the year's bravest act of life-saving.

That particular incident began when the coaster *Orca* developed engine trouble and anchored in St Ives Bay. The tug *Fair Play* arrived from Penzance to tow her away but a nylon hawser wrapped around her propeller and she began to drift helplessly in bad weather. Tommy and his crew arrived on the wings of a force seven to eight northwester, forecasted to worsen, and took off the crew of the tug. It was gusting to force ten and pitch-black when the lifeboat arrived back on scene to rescue the crew of the *Orca*. It was dangerously placed, anchored precariously in the middle of breaking water and due to be dashed against cliffs if its anchor chain broke with the fury of the storm. So, aware of the opinion of the coastguards that the lifeboat would be unable to get out if anything went wrong, Tommy drove his boat into the maelstrom. Not once, but several times – because they could only pick off the crew one at a time.

'We damaged the lifeboat a bit,' says Tommy casually.

But that was nothing compared to the hammering his boat sustained on two other occasions. The first happened in 1977 when he went to search for a boat called the *Lady Camilla* in distress off the Cornish coast with the captain, his wife and two children, and two or three hands on board. The lifeboat was called at midnight and as it launched Eric Kemp, the honorary secretary, came on the beach and said to Tommy: 'Watch your step – it's blowing force twelve!'

They had a fruitless search for the *Lady Camilla* and on the way back in the small hours of the morning another urgent voice spoke in Tommy's ear. It was the second mechanic, Lionel Smith, who said simply: 'Look what's coming!'

'As he said it, I turned around and saw myself looking up at a breaking wave which was between forty and forty-five feet in height. It hit us and we went right over on our beam end. I felt Lionel float past me as I clung on to the spokes of the wheel. When we came up I called out the names of the crew, Lionel first, and thank God they all answered. We had no lifelines in those days but we did have the protection of a canopy. Otherwise I am sure we would have lost a couple of hands overboard.

'When we got back, the medium-frequency radio had gone, so

The 'Grace Darling' lifeboat and three crew members, North Sunderland.

Jane Murphy of Courtmacsherry – training to save lives . . . and souls.

Anne Lawson, first woman to join the 'Grace Darling' crew.

Doris Tart, outside her typical Dungeness dwelling.

Anthony Hawkins – 'Nightmares in Dover'.

A media hero – skipper Jack Woodhouse of the independent Caister lifeboat.

Kelly Allen – a true daughter of Grace Darling.

The old lifeboat house at Lytham St Anne's with an antique windmill in the background.

CREWSAVER
RNLI

Invergordon – Kevin Dent, Sassenach mechanic with oil rig in the far distance.

Courtmacsherry – where support for the lifeboat is total!

had the radar, the radar reflector and the blue flashing light – all washed overboard. It was a real hurricane out there.

'But even that wasn't the worst moment of my lifeboat career. Oddly enough, that came on the very last service I ever did. We were called out to a ship called the *Cecil Japan*, which began to list in bad weather and ran for what he thought was shelter towards a place called Hell's Mouth, around the corner from St Ives Bay. When it did drop anchor it was only about fifty yards off the cliffs. The sea was breaking all over her when we arrived, and the Padstow lifeboat came on the scene too. I tried to get my lifeboat in position to drop anchor and go in on her, and so did the Padstow cox. But neither of us could do it. The conditions were just too bad. Apart from anything else, the *Cecil Japan* had a deck cargo and if that came loose as we were alongside trying to get the crew off it could have been another Penlee job – lifeboat and all aboard her gone.

'Anyway, a helicopter managed to rescue the crew and we were recalled to station. It was a bit dodgy, but when I saw the white light of the Godrevy Lighthouse I said to the crew: "We're all right now, we're on the way home."

'Exactly as I said that, Eric Ward, the man who took over from me when I retired, shouted: "No we aren't – have a look at that coming at us!"

'It was a wall of water forty feet high. I thought, No – not again! We hit it stem on, going at full speed. The lifeboat stopped dead just like hitting a brick wall. When we came out of it we had gone round 180 degrees. There was another one coming and we managed to come up around to it, but that one turned us another 180 degrees. It happened a third time, but through keeping the propellers turning full speed we managed to get out of the breaking water. But I realised there was something wrong with the old girl because she wasn't lifting her bow like she should. So when we arrived back I began to drain the tanks of water – normal procedure – and the first one took twenty minutes to empty instead of two or three seconds. I knew that meant something was seriously wrong, so I phoned the RNLI boat surveyor and inspector and asked them to come down to look at her because I didn't think she was seaworthy any more. She had gone past her time.

'They thought I was stupid. But when they examined her they found all her bulkheads had burst and underneath she was full from stem to stern with water. If we had gone out in her again and she had capsized she wouldn't have been able to right herself.

'So me and the old *Frank Penfold Marshall*, we retired together.'

Tommy won two silver medals for valour during his career. His grandfather collected four awards – one silver, two bronze, and a gold medal from the Hungarian government after a rescue involving one of their merchant vessels. Tommy is still at sea most days, fishing alone for mackerel in his small boat, and says he doesn't miss the status and excitement of his old job.

But as Tommy Cocking relinquished that much-prized position, the family tradition has been maintained. The mechanic and second cox of the St Ives lifeboat is – Tommy Cocking, his son. The second mechanic is William Cocking, another son.

Four generations of Cocking, reaching back most of the century, have now served in the St Ives lifeboat. A true lifeboat dynasty. And there is a grandson, who – naturally – was christened Thomas. So that amazing continuity of service may yet be further stretched.

In complete contrast to the Cocking family saga, if there was ever a man who seemed one of the least likely to become a lifeboat cox, then it is Peter Thompson. Although born in Whitby where a lifeboat station has flourished since 1802, all he wanted to be was a trumpet player. And when total coincidence led him later in life to consider a career in the lifeboat service, his father objected strenuously.

But Peter Thompson became a celebrated cox, and he claims that The Beatles and their ilk were basically responsible!

'I was a professional trumpet player from leaving school. And when I was due for National Service at the age of eighteen in 1956 I applied to serve as a bandsman, and was persuaded to sign on for six years with the Royal Engineers Staff Band. My main interest was big band music, not the military kind, so when I came out I bought a guesthouse in Whitby and worked as a danceband musician all around Yorkshire and Teeside.

'But The Beatles and other groups came along and spoiled it all. It was obvious that big bands and trumpet players were becoming redundant, and the time came when I had to look around for alternative employment to supplement my income from the guesthouse. So I became a lifeguard on Whitby beach.

'Coincidentally, that was the very year the first inshore lifeboat was introduced at Whitby. At first I thought I couldn't become involved because I had injured my back years before lifting a car and was sure I wouldn't pass a medical. But they were relying on the beach staff to run the inshore boat and the RNLI inspector persuaded me to try. I was deemed to be fit, did two seasons on the inshore boat and got to know the crew of the big boat as a result.

'In 1970, the station mechanic retired. Since I was known to be handy with engines, I was asked to apply for the job, which was full time. By then I had caught the lifeboatman's disease – it gets into the blood, you know. Although the pay was only twelve pounds a week, peanuts really, I decided to consider it seriously.

'But when I told my father he wouldn't entertain the idea – and he was the honorary secretary. Over his dead body, he said, because he didn't like the prospect of father and son in key positions with the same lifeboat. So that seemed to be that. However, a week later, he called to see me and said that he had given the matter much thought and concluded that if I wanted to make a career with the RNLI he would not stand in my way. If I still wanted the job, he would inform the inspector. When they appointed me I believe I was the first non-fisherman ever to become a Whitby lifeboatman. And I had no idea about navigation, although I had been on boats owned by my father when I was a boy.

'I served for seven years as the mechanic, then became second cox at an unexpectedly early date because our old Watson boat was replaced by the Waveney, which was based on an American coastguard boat design. People criticised it, said it was more like a glorified cabin cruiser, and most of the fishermen in our crew didn't like it at all. The forty-one-foot Watson handled in a very similar way to their own boats – same speed, same manoeuvrability. Then suddenly they were confronted with this thing which could do sixteen knots – twice as fast as the Watson. It was a completely different concept of lifeboat work.

'All but two of the fishermen in the crew quit when the Waveney arrived. One of them, Bobby Allen, was made cox, and I became second in command. We had to quickly train up some of the inshore crew to work on the new big boat.'

Strangely enough, the Whitby crew were back in a Watson again when they engaged in one of the most dramatic services in the recent history of the RNLI. It happened on 30 September 1976. Two days beforehand their Waveney had lost an engine in a bad weather call-out and was taken out of service. The temporary replacement turned out to be a Watson.

'So there we were back in the old eight-knot boat, with no radar or any modern refinements at all and a five-man crew trained up on a Waveney. Still, it didn't seem at first as though there would be a problem – a Scarborough trawler had gone aground near Saltwick Bay but was expecting to float off with the tide. But it turned out to be stuck in the worst possible place, right on a rock strata called "Kill Me Quick Shaft". It wasn't a bad night to begin with, hardly any wind, but a hell of a swell caused by a previous gale plus a thick fog.

'We sat there for about an hour talking on the radio to the five men on board who, as the weather grew worse, decided they were unlikely to move on their own and asked us to take them off. Bobby, the cox, turned the boat round, dropped the anchor and tried to veer her in through the breaking waves which were rising up to twelve feet by that time.

'On the first run in, the sea began to break over us and it became pretty obvious we weren't going to get anywhere near the vessel because the tide was taking us sideways and washing us further down the coast. But we managed to manoeuvre almost abeam of her and tried firing rocket lines. One went across the top of her rigging but by that time it was so bad that the crew couldn't even get out of the wheelhouse to grab the lines. Their radio was dead, their lights had gone out, the swell was getting bigger and they were in desperate trouble.

'Next thing we had our own crisis when the lifeboat's anchor chain broke. We ended up being washed on to some rocks, slamming into them with Bobby shouting at me to open up on both throttles. Everything was boiling. We were smashed by vertical waves and we thought we had had it. Bobby had the wheel hard over, gradually got her head to the wind and we just about clawed our way out of it. Strangely, at the back of those breakers there was a calm, oily patch where another trawler was standing off – just laid there, no problem. We went alongside him and he gave us a huge fisherman's anchor to replace the one we lost. We put this down, and went in to try again. This time we got a bit closer, but there was no sign of life on the casualty. As it happened, two of the crew had already been washed out to their deaths.

'Suddenly, a large wave hit the bow and one of our crew on the anchor rope was swept the full length of the lifeboat and straight into the stern rails, dislocating his shoulder. Another crewman on the foredeck cracked his head badly at the same time, so we had two really nasty injuries. We took them back to the trawler in the calm spot. Our inshore boat had turned up by this time and the crew were waiting on the trawler to give a hand. It would have been suicide to try going in themselves in their rubber boat. Two of them replaced the injured men and we tried yet again. It was hopeless. We were forced to cut away the big anchor when we were swamped and turned broadside on. Anyway, it turned out all the trawler crew were forced into the sea. Two of them were fortunate enough to make it to the shore alive, but the skipper had ended up clinging to a pinnacle of rock three hundred yards from the cliffs. He was to spend the rest of the night there, with the sea getting bigger and bigger. At the time we had no idea of his predicament, but when daylight came we spotted him. So had the coastguards on the shore and they were trying to rescue him by firing rocket lines, and had got an inshore boat standing by. I told Bobby that the only way we would get him was with the inshore boat so we had a chat on the radio with the helmsman, Richard Robinson, explaining that if he could get into the bay, around the back of the pinnacle and grab the skipper, he could then come out through the surf to join us. There was no chance of going the other way.

'Richard and his crew shot off into the bay and we lost sight of them. For a few tense minutes nothing happened, then we suddenly saw this little orange thing peeping up over the breakers, which were fifteen feet high by this time.

'It was the inshore boat, and they had got the skipper. It hadn't been easy and the inflatable had been slammed against the pinnacle, placing the crew in grave danger themselves, but they had him. The man had survived against all the odds. It was a good moment watching them bounce through the surf to us, and then we all went home.'

Bobby Allen was awarded the RNLI's silver medal, Richard Robinson got a bronze and all the other crew members involved were commended for their extreme courage. Later that same year, Peter Thompson took over as cox and went on to win his own medal, once again demonstrating valour in the highest traditions of the service.

The drama began when two doctors from Leeds left Whitby

harbour in a yacht one morning, bound for Hull – against all sound advice. The sea conditions were perilous in the aftermath of a force eight northerly, and as the yacht passed the harbour bridge the staff were waving and shouting for it to turn back, but it pressed on. Not long after it reached the open sea the yacht was simply overwhelmed and driven towards Whitby Rock and into the shoals underneath the Abbey, where the seas break for half a mile when the weather is bad, a lifeboatman's worst scenario.

'We knew it was a panic job from the start. Someone had kept an eye on the yacht and watched it capsize. The inshore boat was also summoned because it was reported that someone was in the water. We both raced out and the inshore spotted a man in the sea and went straight to him. The yacht was among the breakers, having rolled over twice, and we started looking around for the other man. Then one of the lads shouted that he could see him – hanging off the stern on his lifeline, which was clipped to the yacht. It was obvious it was a life-or-death matter, and no time to play with. He had no energy left, and wasn't going to last long in those conditions. Nor was there much water to work in. A very bad situation all round.

'I had to head towards Whitby Rock, the most dangerous place. I can remember thinking: This is wrong – I'm going to lose this boat! Because the sea was behind us, each wave that hit us pushed us closer to losing control. So I turned the boat round and headed to sea, then went full astern between the waves to try and catch up with the yacht which was still being driven towards the cliffs.

'When I got close enough to make the first bid to get at him, the lifeboat was lifted up and dropped down almost on top of the masts and rigging. I gave the engines a quick burst to get clear, move uptide of him a bit, and then came down with men on the welldeck ready to grab him. It took two or three attempts but we eventually managed to haul him aboard.

'He survived, but his friend was drowned. It was a tragedy which could have been avoided and the whole thing only lasted for fifteen minutes, from start to finish.'

Peter Thompson retired as cox in September 1993, and now runs one of the most successful RNLI museums and shops in the old lifeboat house on the edge of Whitby harbour. His annual turnover has already topped £80,000. In words and pictures the museum tells the heroic history stretching over almost two centuries of one of the most active lifeboat stations of them all. And like so many long established stations it has paid the price. In 1861, the Whitby lifeboat capsized, and all the crew save one were drowned.

Curiously enough, like the sole survivor of the St Ives disaster his name was Freeman – Henry Freeman. And he went on to become coxswain.

12

The Daughters of Grace Darling . . .

If you took a poll among feminists to establish their most inspirational role model, the odds are that Grace Darling would top the list. Her name is writ large in the nation's roll of honour, on equal terms with heroes of the opposite gender, and the image of this handsome young woman bending to the oars of her storm-tossed rowing boat, as romantically portrayed by several artists, is familiar to millions.

Grace Darling secured her permanent place in history on the morning of 7 September 1838. She was the twenty-two-year-old daughter of William Darling, keeper of the Longstone Lighthouse off the far coast of Northumberland, and she rowed that vulnerable boat with her father through the maelstrom, not once but twice, to rescue nine shipwrecked souls stranded on a reef. Within weeks she had been established as a national celebrity, with newspaper reports suggesting that it was she, and not her father, who took the initiative in the epic enterprise. The London *Times*, in a leading article, proclaimed: 'Is there in the whole field of history, or of fiction even, one instance of female heroism to compare with one moment of this?'

Grace was showered with medals and honours, artists queued to paint her likeness, she was pestered by waves of visitors, and even marriage proposals, and offered lucrative theatrical engagements (including one to appear in *Wreck at Sea* at the Adelphi Theatre in London). Commemorative china models and mugs poured off the production line, and William Wordsworth, no less, headed the list of poets writing paeans in her praise, starting his lines with:

A guardian spirit, sent from pitying heaven,
In woman's shape . . .

The modest manner in which Grace dealt with this potentially destabilising avalanche of attention added further lustre to her status. She turned down all offers to parade herself and scarcely touched a subscription fund (to which Queen Victoria personally sent fifty pounds). Within four years she was dead, a victim of tuberculosis. In its own sad way, that doubtless helped to ensure that her name would live on. No chance for public or press to perceive, or invent, frailties in later years, and they would surely have been watching closely. There are suggestions that her state of health was made worse by the persistent curiosity of an endless stream of visitors, including journalists.

To those who recognise the truth in the saying that a prophet often hath no honour in his or her own land, it will come as no surprise to learn that the one place where admiration for Grace Darling was not unanimous happened to be in that part of Northumberland where she was born and raised. Research among informed local opinion suggests that there was some resentment among the fishermen of Seahouses and Bamburgh. They felt that Grace and her father should have left the rescue to them, because it was usual to secure a handsome reward from grateful survivors.

They also took offence at the enormous fame lavished upon Grace, and probably regarded the subscriptions with some envy.

Fittingly, however, at North Sunderland (situated in Seahouses, but so called because that place didn't exist when the RNLI set up shop in 1827), the lifeboat is called the *Grace Darling*. Today, the RNLI is keen to keep the flame lit by their prime asset burning brightly. Although some coxes will not allow females to join their crew – examples are confirmed in Cornwall and the Western Highlands – barriers are starting to crumble elsewhere. At the time of writing there are more than eighty women officially listed at the headquarters in Poole, Dorset, as RNLI crew members – including one in the North Sunderland boat.

They have been made particularly welcome, for instance, at Courtmacsherry Harbour in County Cork in the Republic of Ireland. There are no fewer than four women in the crew and the first one that joined has an especially interesting background. Jane Murphy is concerned not only in rescuing lives, but also in saving souls.

She is training to be a nun, and was recently absent from lifeboat duties because she is working with deprived children in Ethiopia. She demonstrated her courage on her very first working day with the lifeboat when a cabin door slammed and broke her hand. It did not deter her for one moment. She is obviously descended from sterling stock since her uncle was a petty officer on HMS *Amethyst*, the Royal Naval frigate which famously ran the gauntlet of Communist Chinese guns as it escaped down the Yangtze River in 1949, defiantly returning fire as it did so. The newspapers were ecstatic about this Nelsonian act.

The other three Courtmacsherry women have family connections with the local lifeboat. Patricia Gannon is the wife of mechanic Mark, and she also shares in the running of their pleasure boats in the summer season. Sisters Oonagh and Eadine Hickey, are daughters of the lifeboat's medical officer, Matthias Hickey. Both girls are pursuing professional careers, one as an accountant, and the other training to follow in her father's footsteps.

They all say the prospect of adventure and the satisfaction of being part of a skilled team attracted them to the lifeboat, and they are clearly prepared to share the discomforts since at least one of them has been flung overboard in life jacket tests. They have taken part in other exercises and are all keen to see real action.

Matthias Hickey is quick to take issue with anyone who suggests that the lifeboat service should be an exclusively male preserve.

'It's equality of the sexes these days, and I am very proud of my daughters. From a medical point of view, I think the weakest part of any person serving on a lifeboat is their stomach – in other words, susceptibility to seasickness. Mr Perfect, with a body rippling with muscle, can be reduced to the consistency of a jellyfish. These girls do not get seasick. My two daughters accompany me regularly on fishing trips and they have a very good head for the sea.'

The women of Seahouses were certainly expected to cope with some tough work in the past, as Thomas Dawson, the elder statesman of the North Sunderland lifeboat, freely admits. Now well into his eighties, he fished for a living like his forefathers and served long years on the lifeboat, the last sixteen as cox.

'It was hard for us all in Seahouses when I was a boy, with large families and very little money. But the womenfolk had the worst of it during the wintertime when we used to fish with long lines, 1,200 hooks to a line. Families had to get up at five in the morning to collect mussels and limpets, scraping them from the rocks, before shelling them and placing them on the hooks for bait. It was rough work, and the women had to do it. The kids helped, of course – and there were plenty of them. I had five sisters and four brothers. It was usual for one woman to do 600 spare hooks in the morning, and 600 more when her menfolk came in from the sea for their food. The houses had no bathrooms, no electricity or water on tap, but everyone had a large kitchen!'

There appear to be no descendants of Grace Darling around in Seahouses and Bamburgh these days. But one remarkable person arrived early in 1995 to carry the banner Grace raised more than a century and a half ago.

Anne Jeanette Lawson projects just the right kind of adventurous image required for a well-scrutinised role as the very first female member of the *Grace Darling* crew. She is athletic, a qualified pilot with a share in a light plane and a descendant of lifeboatmen on each side of the family. She was born in 1960 in the Midlands, though both her grandfathers were Northeastern seafarers. One was a fisherman in South Shields, the other a pilot on the Tyne river who superintended the progress of the *Mauritania* as that famous vessel left on her maiden voyage.

She is clearly accustomed to dealing with trauma since she was widowed after less than six months of marriage. She trained as a microbiologist but opted for a business career, opening a shop in Seahouses in 1983. Now the proprietor of a local caravan site, her appointment proved to be a very newsworthy event. She was besieged by reporters.

As the assembled media wait expectantly for Anne Lawson to take part in a newsworthy mission, women were already well established in 42 of the 210 lifeboat stations, a 20 per cent rating. No medals to date but there will no doubt be a media explosion if and when that happens. Grace Darling was awarded three, including a silver from the National Institution for the Preservation of Life from Shipwreck, which later became the RNLI, and a gold from the Royal Humane Society.

Which one of her daughters will be the first to follow suit?

13

. . . and a Child of Neptune

Kelly Allen is a bonny lass only just old enough to vote. But she is already a worthy daughter of Grace Darling – and a true child of Neptune to boot. It is doubtful in the extreme if anyone can match her precocious record of service in the RNLI.

Kelly has been wedded to sea from childhood, which she spent almost exclusively around the harbour at Portrush, in County Antrim, Northern Ireland. As the tragic sectarian conflict raged close by – occasionally very close – she applied all her youthful enthusiasm to absorbing the ways of the sea. She learned to sail on top of it, then at fifteen was initiated into diving under it by her father. Already qualified as a dive leader, she will shortly be recognised as an instructor. And just to confirm her aquatic nature, Kelly has also formed a deep bond with a bottlenose dolphin.

Even in her bucket and spade days Kelly was drawn to the lifeboat, and as she entered her teens she would watch enthralled as it roared out of the harbour on rescue missions. A wistful ambition was created.

'I thought I would like to be part of that, but was convinced they would never allow a girl to join the crew. I even wished I was a boy!'

But she cleverly developed a very useful ally, the wise and experienced John Scott, who had served in the Portrush lifeboat for many years before becoming the honorary secretary. Kelly got to know him well at the yacht club and, when the time came, enquired about her chances of joining the crew. John Scott was impressed.

'Not only did she know about sailing and diving, but I realised that she was the sort of kid who would get stuck into a job. She had the right attitude and didn't mind doing the dirty jobs, such as lying on her back to scrub the bottom of a boat. When she was coming up to her seventeenth birthday I arranged an RNLI medical and told her there might be a place in the inshore boat. Since then she has become a real asset, well able to take the ribbing the lads gave her. But they do respect her.'

The girl herself remembers very well the day she became a crew member.

'The others knew that something was happening, and I was so worried in case they didn't like the idea. I just kind of hid myself away to begin with, then I was told to attend my first crew meeting. That was before I had been on the boat, and it was awful. I had to walk in as they were all sitting there, staring at me.

'At first they thought I wouldn't be able to do everything they could so I had to try and prove them wrong!'

And so she did. Her very first service, early in 1994, was traumatic enough to make any youngster, male or female, cry quits. Kelly made up a three-man (or person!) crew which went out on the inshore to search for a sixteen-year-old boy on a Sunday school outing to West Bay, alongside Portrush, who had gone for a swim and disappeared.

'When we arrived we thought it was a hoax because the beach was empty. But the coastguard assured us that someone was missing, and we searched for ages. It was quite rough that day with a lot of swell. The big boat was turned out and the helicopter, too. We were operating in the surf where the big boat couldn't go when the helicopter dropped an orange flare. That meant they had spotted a body. When we got to the place I was the first one to see it. But the moment I called out a wave caught us, washed our boat into the beach and we lost it. A few minutes later we saw it again, right under us. He was near the sea bed and wearing blue swimming trunks. There were three of us in the boat and one of us had to get out, try and pick him up. It was almost impossible because we were wearing life jackets and he was about ten feet under water, and all the time the swell was throwing the boat around. Eventually two of us went duck diving, and the crewman in the water with me finally grabbed him. I went back in the boat to help pull the boy in, and he was sick all over me. It was horrible. We tried resuscitation, but he was dead.

'The experience didn't put me off. I know you have to deal with things like that if you want to be in the lifeboat crew. I was OK but some of the men felt sick. However, it was a long time before I could get the picture of that poor boy out of my head.'

John Scott was very worried about Kelly's reaction to such a nightmare introduction to the lifeboat service and hurried to counsel her.

'I asked her if she was all right, and the answer I got was: "There was a job to do, John, and we did it." Quite amazing!'

During the summer of 1994, there were over thirty callouts for the inshore lifeboat at Portrush and Kelly made most of them. She says she almost made herself unpopular with the rest of the crew because, since she haunts the harbour every summer, she was always first there when the bleepers went off.

'They accused me of just hanging around waiting for a call. And yet on one occasion I missed a call, and still ended up helping to rescue two people. I had gone off for the day in a private boat with another crew member down the coast to Port Ballintrae. We were messing around in the harbour in our wet suits, jumping off the pier and swimming about when our bleepers went off. Since we were fifteen minutes away I didn't think we had any chance of making it, but we still set off at speed on the boat to see what was happening. When we came round the head into Portrush Bay where the incident was supposed to be taking place we couldn't see the inshore boat anywhere. However, we did see the coastguard's van on the shore and then spotted two swimmers panicking in the water. They were screaming and shouting and very cold. Apparently, the inshore boat had been given the wrong position and had shot off in another direction, so we picked them out. It turned out I knew them – they were two girls from my own school. They were in a pretty bad way, too, suffering from cramp and almost unconscious.'

Kelly herself once got into serious difficulties whilst swimming in the sea and was fortunate enough to be rescued. Not by a lifeboat, however. By a dolphin. No other sea dweller has such historic associations with man as the dolphin. The ancient Greeks deified them, to the Minoans they were the symbol of happiness, and today there is a body of opinion which believes they are endowed with therapeutic qualities. Whenever a wild dolphin begins to associate freely with humans – and it often happens – people who suffer from a range of nervous disorders are brought to swim with them.

In most cases there appears to be a very beneficial effect. There have also been several recorded incidents of dolphins helping to rescue people.

In recent years, several solitary dolphins have taken up offshore residence around the coasts of Britain and Ireland. They come and go, but there is frequently one available and willing to frolic with people. One of the most celebrated arrived in Dingle Bay, on the far west coast of the Republic of Ireland, in the eighties. Kelly has fallen under its spell.

'I went down to Dingle Bay with my family to meet him when I was really young, and I just went crazy about dolphins. So we go every year now. He's a bottlenosed dolphin called Fungi and he seems to have taken a real liking to me, because he is always around me when I go swimming in the bay.

'One day I was playing with Fungi when the tide turned very strongly and I began to be swept out of the bay. My uncle was in the boat so I shouted out to him to come and pick me up, because I was tiring fast. But he couldn't start the engine. I saw him pulling and pulling, but he was getting smaller and smaller. It took him about fifteen minutes to start it. I was very concerned because I happen to know there isn't a lifeboat station for miles.

'But Fungi stayed with me the whole time. He let me hold on to him and then pulled me back into the bay. When Uncle arrived to haul me out, he just disappeared. It was wonderful.'

Kelly is studying design to A level standard at the moment and has thoughts about going to university in England. This will inevitably halt her lifeboat career, but only on a temporary basis if she has her way. Once she has established herself in a job – she aims at photography or graphics – she intends to resume lifeboat service and hopes to be allowed to go on the main boat.

'In fact, I'd like to be involved with the lifeboat for the rest of my life.'

One day, perhaps, a woman may be appointed the cox of a lifeboat. Keep your eye on Kelly Allen!

14

The Tarts of Dungeness

Arriving for the first time in Dungeness, after proceeding through the traditional seaside architecture of Hastings or Folkestone, does come as a distinct culture shock. Somehow it doesn't appear to belong in this prim and prosperous slice of southern England. The place hangs precariously on a sparse and lonely lip of the Kent coast which juts defiantly out into the English Channel, challenging the wind and sea to do its worst. And there is no shelter here from the elements. An overdeveloped seaside community it certainly is not. Pancake-flat, it is dotted with tiny, single-storey houses, each haphazardly set in its own parcel of land, as if a giant hand had scooped up a score or two of chalets from one of the very early holiday camps and scattered them loosely around. There appear to be no centre or shops or school or similar community assets of any kind apart from a pub. But a very narrow railway track winds bizarrely between the dwellings, just yards away from some front doors, as though the giant brought along his Hornby set. He would have needed something to divert him, for Dungeness is not an exciting place. It seems to have been asleep for a few decades. And the emptiness is quite eerie.

Now speaking in comparative terms, a giant does reside there. Rising high above the neighbouring rooftops and dominating the landscape, it must be quite possible to fit half a dozen of those dolls' houses inside the place and still have room for a dance floor. This is the Dungeness lifeboat house.

And it is the lifeboat which over the last century and a half has brought distinction to this curious little community. Indeed, it has brought forth a certain name which, since the turn of the century, has burnished the image of the numerous women who work on the fringes of lifeboat society everywhere: the Tarts of Dungeness.

These women did not win their fame by just making hot drinks for their menfolk as they returned from lifeboat service, or selling souvenirs in the station shop. The Tarts of Dungeness were very formidable, able to face danger and use muscle like the toughest mariner. In all weathers, they launched the boat from the beach and then pulled it back up again on its return.

The Tarts are still flourishing in Dungeness, and one of them, Mrs Sis Tart, explained why it was necessary for women to undertake such a difficult, and occasionally dangerous task.

'It's only ever been a small population here – around 200 these days – and most of the available men were in the lifeboat crew. So it was up to the women to launch. There was just no alternative. First, we laid greasy poles under the lifeboat as it went down the beach, then recovered them as it hit the water. Heavy things they were, too. Getting the boat back out of the water and into the shed was the really hard part, because we didn't have a motorised winch in those days. We had to push a big capstan with bars stuck through it, winding the tow wire around the barrel. There were usually about half a dozen Tart women in the team, mostly wives of the crew. The other main families around here have always been the Oilers and the Richardsons.'

Sis Tart possesses a newspaper cutting dated 1932, which shows that this Dungeness sisterhood was already basking in national fame more than sixty years ago. The report describes a launch when 'a sudden gust of wind blew the boat right off the skids on to the beach . . . the gallant women of Dungeness were wet to the skin and hardly able to keep their feet on the loose stones . . . but they got the lifeboat away on the second attempt.'

The newspaper lists some of their names: 'Mrs J. Tart, Mrs A. Tart, Mrs A. Oiler, Mrs T. Oiler, Mrs Richardson . . . etc.' – and says that the Tarts and Oilers had been putting the lifeboat to sea for nearly twenty-five years – which means that they were doing it long before the start of the First World War.

Sis Tart was born a Richardson and came to Dungeness at the age of four when her lifeboatman father, Charlie, had one of the little bungalows built. That was eighty-five years ago, and this remarkably agile lady is on the verge of her ninety-first year.

That the Dungeness dwellings were constructed from asbestos and matchwood and a nuclear power station lurks nearby seems to have done her no harm at all. She cuts a dashing figure on her moped when she goes shopping or visiting friends, but she is quick to point out that she always wears the correct headgear! Sis, a widow for nearly twenty years, married Ben Tart, known as Punch, who joined the Dungeness lifeboat at the age of seventeen and served as cox for eighteen years. The family connection continues, for her grandson, David Tart, is in the crew and her nephew, Patrick Richardson, is the full-time mechanic and second cox. The cox is William Richardson.

Ben Tart won a bronze medal in July 1956, for a rescue which still echoes in the memory of his widow, and dramatically points up the stress that lifeboat wives often have to endure.

'I was frightened. All the women were frightened. It was a terrible, terrible day. A coaster called the *Teeswood*, with a crew of about ten, was trying to sail around the point but it became too much for it and when it turned to come into the bay for shelter it capsized. When we launched our lifeboat, the retired cox, Doug Oiler, was very worried. He didn't think they would come back. He didn't suggest they shouldn't go – he would never do that because nothing is too bad for the lifeboat.

'That day I had four members of my family on the lifeboat – my husband, who was cox, my eldest son, my brother and my brother-in-law. They were out there for two hours. A big tanker appeared and proceeded to pour oil on the waves to smooth them down, but unfortunately some of the men who had jumped into the water swallowed some of the oil and it made them very ill. But they all recovered except one. That was the cook, who was pulled out and one of our men tried very hard to revive him but I'm afraid he died.

'And, would you believe, as soon as they came ashore there was another Mayday because there happened to be a big yacht race on in the Channel at the time and there were boats in trouble all over the place. Altogether, our boat was out for twenty-four hours. Countess Mountbatten presented my husband with his bronze medal.'

One of Sis Tart's close neighbours, Albert 'Honker' Haines took part in the *Teeswood* rescue, and he, now rising eighty, served almost forty years in the Dungeness lifeboat. He succeeded Sis's husband as cox and stayed in command until his retirement in 1978.

The miniature railway runs within a few feet of his front door, now used mainly for the benefit of tourists, but he remembers its being employed in a novel manner in the defence of the nation during the last war. The shoreline around Dungeness was obviously vulnerable to enemy attack from the sea so someone had the bright idea of mounting a gun on one of the carriages, so it could be deployed swiftly to the best position. It had other uses, too.

'Yes, very handy it was. We got to know the army boys and they would pick us up at the pub and drop us off where we lived!'

Honker nominated a wartime tragedy as the worst incident of his long career in the lifeboat. A fishing trawler which had been appropriated by the Royal Navy and equipped with a barrage balloon went ashore to the west of Dungeness. Bureaucracy agonisingly conspired with a southerly gale with fateful consequences, as Honker recalled with much sadness.

'We weren't called soon enough. In those days you had to wait for permission from the Admiralty. When we arrived seven men had already decided to try and save themselves by swimming ashore. They drowned. Those who waited tied ropes around their waists for us to grab, and jumped in.'

The cox on that mission was Doug Oiler, another man with more than four decades of service in the lifeboat, and his daughter, now in her mid-seventies, currently lives within hailing distance of Honker Haines. She became Mrs Doris Tart, which naturally led to membership of that famously courageous team.

'I helped to launch the lifeboat for about thirty-five years. It was hard work, particularly on a low-water launch when twenty skids would be needed. They were heavy oak, not plastic, so you didn't have to worry about your fingernails! Getting the boat out again was even worse. We would be wet through and freezing, sometimes for two hours at a time, but funnily enough never once did I become ill because of launching. I didn't even catch as much as a cold in all those years.'

The man she married, Tom Tart – known for unspecified reasons as Ben – is the senior surviving lifeboatman in Dungeness. Now past his eightieth year and not in good health, he succeeded his first cousin, 'Punch' Tart (real name, curiously, Ben), as coxswain.

He won a silver medal in February 1974, when the boat was called out in a hurricane to bring a seriously injured man off the Danish motor vessel *Merc Texco*. The conditions were too bad for a helicopter to take off, so the man's only hope was the lifeboat. It was a nightmare launch, as Doris Tart explained.

'Twice we tried to get her away, but she was thrown right up on end and swept back to the beach. The launchers decided that it was going to be impossible, and were preparing to put a wire on to haul her out. We thought we couldn't let her be pounded up and down in the surf any more. But my husband ordered us to have one more go, and just managed to motor her through the waves and away.

'When they came alongside the *Merc Texco* they discovered that the man hadn't been prepared to go. So a very young member of our crew, Peter Thomas, volunteered to board her. He was such a brave boy because it was so hazardous. Both boats were pitching violently up and down and he had to time it just right to leap safely aboard. But he made it, got the casualty strapped into a stretcher, and organised a transfer, which was just as risky.

'It was so rough on the way back that crew members had to kneel down alongside the stretcher and hang on to keep it steady. The man survived. My husband got his silver, and Peter received a richly deserved bronze medal.'

15

A Price to Pay

Many lifeboatmen have paid a heavy price for their devotion to their courageous calling. For most, it was swift oblivion in raging seas. But for Alfred Pavey, former cox of the Weymouth lifeboat, who has a sparkling personality and reputation which led to a *This Is Your Life* appearance, it has been an excruciatingly slow and painful process. He has been paying the price for more than a quarter of a century.

'The trouble was, you see, those old boats had no shelter. You were often wet through before you left the harbour and had to sit in it for hour after hour. It all began for me with a pain in my big toe when I was about forty years old. Then it suddenly shot into my two wrists. Arthritis, of course. I had it for a long time before they found out. But I eventually needed to go into hospital for an operation, and that was the end of me. The old coxes didn't have to retire until they were sixty-five, but I had to go in 1978 when I was only fifty-three.

'Looking back now, I realise I should have gone earlier. I was used to the old lifeboats that did nine knots, which meant that if you went to the top of a big sea you would usually come down gently on the other side. Very rarely did you fall down heavily. That changed when the new boats arrived. They are so fast. I would have been wise to retire in 1975 when we were given one, because the first time I took her out we ran into an easterly gale off Falmouth. It went up a wave, and came down with such force that my knees came up to the top of my head! That's what it felt like anyway.

'So there it was. I didn't want to go, but they sent me a letter saying I ought to. I had to have plastic knees, which meant that if I had fallen over in the boat and broken them where they are joined to the original bone I would have been crippled for life.

'Fourteen operations I've been through. My hands and my shoulders are so bad now that more surgery has been suggested. But I said I feel I've had enough and I'll put up with the pain unless I can't stand it any more. I'm not so young as I was when I started all this, but I will go ahead and damn the consequences if necessary.

'I have been told that but for this arthritis there would be nothing wrong with me. An absolutely fit man, otherwise!'

Ironically, Alf Pavey had a flying start to his senior career in the lifeboat service. He was appointed coxswain of the Weymouth boat in 1962, when he was only thirty-five, the youngest cox around the south coast.

'In those days you rarely became cox until you were in your forties, and the local RNLI inspector said I was too young. But I insisted I could do it.'

There is no doubt that Alf had the skills for the job. In fact, he was probably the best qualified young seaman around the Weymouth area at the time. He had returned from military service after extensive training and experience in navigation and seamanship. In the army!

'I did ask to go in the navy when they called me up, since I came from a fishing family going back many generations, but I was sent off to the army. The war was still on at the time. However, it worked out well for me because they put me on the army boats – the Royal Army Service Corps Water Transport – delivering stores and supplies to all the forts along the coasts. That's how I had my formal education in seamanship. The old Weymouth men had no idea about that sort of thing . . . they smelled their way about! To tell the truth I think some of them couldn't even use a compass, but they certainly knew their way around the fishing grounds. And in the early days they went out dredging for scallops in open twenty-one-footers, driven by old car engines. My dad's engine had no reverse gear on it – it only drove ahead. Money was too scarce then to afford anything else because the price we were getting for our fish was ridiculously low. I recall delivering plaice with a mate to a local fishmonger, who was paying us twenty-one shillings [£1.05] a stone – fourteen pounds weight. As we were leaving a lady came in, pointed at our plaice and asked for two. "Certainly, madam," said the fishmonger. "That'll be twelve shillings [60p]." Right in front of us!

'Those army boats were vastly different to the kind I had been brought up to. They were fifty-two feet long with a hold in the middle and accommodation for the crew. I learned about coastal navigation and then how to handle a boat in the best training ground of them all – the Thames. The tide in that river is very powerful and there is so much traffic – like Piccadilly Circus on water sometimes.

'By the time I was nineteen, I was Corporal Pavey, coxswain of my boat and in command of a crew of four.

'I came back home to Weymouth when the war ended. I was twenty-one, with the world at my feet. My father died young, at the age of fifty-two, and I took over the family business – two boats used for mackerel fishing and taking tourists for trips. There was a bit more prosperity by then, and plenty of employment. In 1948 I was asked to join the lifeboat crew.'

For the next thirty years Alf Pavey was the centre of numerous hair-raising rescue missions. Portland Bill is on the Weymouth patch and the lifeboat often had to run the gauntlet of the seven tides that meet there to whip the sea into a frenzy, the fearsome Portland Race. In 1971, he won a bronze for going out in a hurricane to a lone yachtsman who had been thrown about so violently that his ribs were fractured.

'I took a doctor with me. He had just been appointed to the lifeboat crew and it was the first time that poor man had ever been to sea. But he was brave enough to jump aboard that yacht, along with the bowman, when I managed to get alongside it. We put a rope across and began to tow him back to Weymouth, but the rope broke three times – with the doctor and the bowman still on board because it was too fierce to get the casualty on to the lifeboat. Eventually it held long enough to make it back.

'The next day the doctor rang me and said: "I want to thank you for bringing me home safely." I'll never forget those words. Dr Jeremy E. C. Parkinson is his name. And he is my doctor now, treating me for the blessed arthritis.

'The yachtsman, a very decent man from Bournemouth, also came to thank me when he was released from hospital. He even turned up when they did my *This Is Your Life* in 1977. With regard to that event, I always say, taking a cue from Winston Churchill, that never were so many lies told by so few in such a short time! How my wife, Joan, kept it a secret I will never know. It was a wonderful experience.'

Most old lifeboatmen can pluck from their memories a story which, among all the hundreds of uniformly heroic accounts of rescues against the odds, has unique, sometimes bizarre elements. Alf Pavey has an outstanding example.

'It happened during the height of the Cold War. A woman on board a Russian ship going up the channel in a southeasterly had a miscarriage. Now Portland harbour is sheltered from a gale in that direction and the Russian skipper asked permission to go in there. But the navy refused because Portland is a naval base. The only other bit of lee available was east of Portland, so we launched with Dr Gordon Wallace, who preceded Dr Parkinson, and met the Russian boat at a point nine miles offshore. That was the nearest the navy would allow it to approach this country. It seemed to be just a cargo boat and I saw no suspicious antennae like those carried by the spy boats. There was a great swell and I was afraid Dr Wallace would be crushed between the Russian vessel and our lifeboat but he climbed aboard safely.

'The woman turned out to be in a bad way. She was lowered down to us strapped in a stretcher and the doctor told me we must get her ashore as quickly as possible. There was only one way to do that – go straight through the Portland Race. Under normal circumstances you always tried to dodge around the Race, but that puts another five miles on the distance. So we battened down the hatches and went for it. We made it, got her to the hospital in time and she was saved. I believe she may have died if we hadn't taken the quicker way.

'I went to see her the next day and she thanked me through an interpreter. She was in her thirties and I do not know what she was doing on a Russian boat. Maybe she was a cook, or someone's wife.'

The gallant manner in which Alf Pavey has led the Weymouth lifeboat for so long has been continued with conspicuous success by the new management. His successor as cox, Vic Pitman, collected a silver medal, and Derek Sergeant a bronze after he took over command.

16

Nightmares in Dover

By the very nature of their calling, experienced lifeboatmen are obliged to witness sights and situations which would fuel recurring nightmares in most people. The majority can tell stories which chill the blood, none more so than the cox of the Dover lifeboat, Tony Hawkins. He has been at the centre of at least two incidents which are so horrifying that he freely admits that his sleep is troubled by their memory.

The most poignant, perhaps, occurred one winter's night when a ship with a cargo of iron ore ran over a partly submerged wreck in the English Channel and was ripped apart. Tony Hawkins has seen many bodies in the water during his time on the Dover boat, but there is just one which still disturbs him, almost thirty years on.

'He was a young seaman, dressed only in a tee shirt and jeans cut off at the knee. Since it was winter, I imagine he had been asleep, maybe in the engine room. Like the others, he probably got out of his bunk and jumped straight overboard as the boat sank.

'This boy had made it to a life raft container. He must have thought he was going to save his life, but it seems he didn't have the strength to pull the rope which inflates the life raft. He had just got his hand into it and was still holding on when we found him. He had a St Christopher medallion around his neck and wore a watch which had stopped at around 9.40.

'I can still see that bloke there now. It's a sight I will never forget.

'There were other bodies in the water that night – in fact we ended up with about fifteen stacked up around the lifeboat. It was dreadful. It was even difficult to walk around the boat, and I remember treading on someone's hand and apologising to him. I said sorry to a dead man!'

Not a seafaring man in the traditional sense, Tony Hawkins is a production supervisor at a company manufacturing electronic instruments – which just happens to be conveniently located close by Dover harbour. He works for a very understanding management – and if he loses time going off on the lifeboat he makes it good later. He did spend his childhood messing around with boats in St Margaret's Bay, between Dover and Deal, and learned his seamanship at school. His father, George, a publican in the Dover area, was a member of the lifeboat crew and Tony, along with his twin brother, Richard, can claim to have started their service in the lifeboat at a very early age.

'My father was driving us to school one morning when the maroons went off. It turned out they were short-handed so – although we were only fourteen at the time – the cox, Johnny Walker, said we could come along. A great moment. But we had trouble persuading the school to believe our story when we finally turned up.'

Tony left school at the age of sixteen, trained as a marine electronics engineer, and when he qualified spent a lot of time at sea sorting out electronic problems on ships because he was the only one of the team who didn't suffer from seasickness. And following a special arrangement between the local RNLI inspector and their father, who had to sign an agreement accepting responsibility, Tony and his twin were allowed to carry on as under-age members of the Dover crew, when it was deemed both safe and necessary. Both eventually progressed to the top position in the service. Richard became cox of the Great Yarmouth boat.

Their parallel lives have continued in uncanny fashion, because both hold the bronze medal for valour.

Tony won his when the steering of a coaster became jammed and the ship was driven towards the Goodwin Sands. The crew of fifteen began to panic and all they wanted to do was to get off, but the conditions were so atrocious that it would have been very dangerous.

'There were no tugs available so we tried to tell them to get some emergency steering sorted out by rigging up a pulley and tackle on top of the rudder stock in the engine room. There was a language problem because the crew were all foreign, and we had to shout a bit, but calm was eventually established and the message got through to them. They went below and fixed something up. All the time we were assuring them that they wouldn't drown, and that we would stand by and come alongside and take them off if it proved necessary – although, to be frank, I'm not sure that would have been possible.

'When they were ready we told them to pull it about to midships and we would steam ahead and give them instructions about which course to take. In this way we guided them back to Dover and managed to enter the harbour although it was officially closed at the time because of the tremendous seas. It all went on for several hours and I shared the helm with the cox, Arthur Lidden, who was awarded the silver medal for his leadership.'

Tony Hawkins took over as cox in 1979, at the age of thirty-five. His patch includes some of the most hazardous and accident-prone stretches of seaway anywhere in the world and there are usually in excess of fifty calls a year for the Dover lifeboat. The narrow Strait of Dover is congested on a daily basis with ships of all sizes, speeds and nationalities, from hovercraft and jetfoils capable of more than forty knots, cargo vessels and tankers in profusion hurrying along at twenty knots or more, all mixed in with a variety of pleasure craft. Some of them are less than vigilant, and Tony recalls one occasion which features high in the long list of incidents which still haunt him.

'We were in dense fog, towing a cabin cruiser back from the Goodwin Sands. We had asked the coastguards to broadcast a general message to all vessels that we were coming around the shipping lanes, giving our position and saying that we had restricted mobility because of the casualty.

'Then we saw an echo on the radar. It was closing . . . and kept on closing. We tried to call him on Channel Sixteen, the international frequency, and we got the coastguards to call him too. There was no response.

'I just didn't know what to do. It was coming from aft of us and overtaking. The signal vanished from the screen so I went on deck. Visibility was so bad I couldn't even see the front of the lifeboat, but I could hear his propellers thumping away. All I could do was wait and hope for the best. It must have been very, very close when it passed. We never did identify the boat.'

'Now that's another one which sticks in my mind to this day.'

There have been other incidents, particularly the horrifying accident which happened in Dover harbour in 1985, when the hovercraft *Princess Margaret* collided with the wall.

'I was in the bath when the alarm was given at around four in the afternoon, but we launched within six minutes. Three minutes later we were alongside her. The impact had ripped out the whole of one side, about eighty or ninety feet. There were about twenty people in the water, shouting and screaming, and we actually put the lifeboat into the hole in the side to get at the people trapped in the lower part of the hovercraft.

'It was a frightening sight, and one or two of my crew froze. I had to shout at them to get moving again. We took off five or six of the most seriously injured and brought them ashore before returning. The rest of the passengers were still in their seats, but there was nothing underneath them but water.

'In total, we landed 175 passengers – 115 in one go. There were 5 fatalities.'

Fortunately for his peace of mind, not all Tony Hawkins' experiences on the Dover lifeboat are concerned with death and disaster. There have been some remarkable happy endings, which he recalls with much pleasure.

'One summer afternoon not long ago we went to a small rowing boat reported sinking about five miles off the coast near Folkestone. There were two small boys aboard, one aged about eight, and the other eleven, the sons of a local fisherman. They had pinched the boat their father used to ferry himself to and from his big fishing boat on its moorings, and obviously decided to follow in his footsteps because they had been hauling nets. I approached at about twenty knots and then had to slow down suddenly or I would have swamped them. There were only about three inches of freeboard left because of the weight of the nets, and water had been slopping over the side.

'My lads grabbed the smaller boy, who couldn't move partly because of fright, and partly because his legs were tangled up in the nets. He would have drowned had the boat capsized, no doubt about it. The other one was sitting in the stern, and he was frozen with fear and cold as well. We got them in the cabin and wrapped them up in blankets. I handed over the wheel to one of my crew and went below to have a word with them.

The first thing they said to me was: "You won't tell our dad, will you?"

'I told them that would be difficult to avoid, asked for his name and realised I knew him. We had been at school together. I also assured them I was confident I could persuade him not to give them a good hiding. We arrived in Folkestone, and the father was down on the quay. He was very upset, and very annoyed – at first. Then I reminded him of two things: that we had been at school together, used to sail together in the school boats and . . . we had rescued him in the lifeboat about ten years ago when his fishing boat ran into trouble.

'The crew and myself were so pleased that day. We considered we had done something pretty good. Saved the father and the sons. Very satisfying.

'There was one other outstandingly happy occasion, when we acted totally against RNLI policy. A coastguard phoned me and said rather guardedly that he had a problem and could the lifeboat handle it? He explained that there was an elderly lady on the cliff between Dover and Deal who was going absolutely frantic. Her golden retriever dog had fallen over the cliff. It was still alive, because people could hear it barking and crying. The lady was threatening to jump over the cliff herself if nobody would help. Now you don't launch a lifeboat for an animal, but I agreed to try and get an exercise organised very quickly. I phoned around the crew and the honorary secretary's deputy, and suggested we had an unpaid exercise – say, to test the radar! Then I called a vet I know who fortunately was in his surgery and willing to go. So we launched. When we arrived at the cliff it was low water, so we had to put out the Y boat, the crew's rubber lifeboat, and two crewmen took the vet to the dog. It had broken its pelvis. The vet gave it an injection to ease the pain and it was carried back on a stretcher and put on the main boat.

'The look on the face of that dog when it arrived back in Dover and was reunited with his mistress is something else I will never forget. I know I had tears in my eyes, and that went for a few of my crew, as well.

'It took six weeks, but the dog made a full recovery. We all went to have our photographs taken for the newspapers when it was discharged by the vet. And to this day, we have had more money donated to the RNLI because we rescued that dog than any other job we have done. The lady herself has raised quite a lot of money, too. You know, we often save boats worth up to half a million pounds, and don't even get a thank you.

'The vet donated a muzzle he used that day, just in case it was needed again. It remains part of the equipment we always carry on the Dover lifeboat.'

17

The Deadly Goodwins

They lie in wait for stricken or unwary ships, a maze-like stretch of sandbanks twelve miles in length and around four to five miles in width, which crouch five miles off the coast between Dover and Ramsgate – the Goodwin Sands.

For centuries, ships plying up and down the narrow part of the seas which keep Britain separate from the European mainland, and those heading for the mouth of the Thames and the Port of London, have fallen into the deadly embrace of the Goodwins. Countless thousands of seamen have perished there.

The seafaring men of Kent – fishermen and, particularly, lifeboatmen – are very familiar with the nature of this beast. And yet its treacherous complexity can still trap even the wisest and most experienced. One family has fought a pitched battle with the Goodwins for at least four generations, and probably a few more. The Cannons of Ramsgate have traditionally both sought a living and saved many lives from the sea, and the latest in the line is Ron Cannon, coxswain mechanic of the Ramsgate lifeboat.

'My great-great-grandfather was a Ramsgate fisherman, and since fishing and the lifeboat have always gone hand in hand in this community it is likely that Cannons have served in the lifeboat ever since it was founded in 1802.'

The Ramsgate lifeboat is the senior Kent station, preceding the next in line, Dungeness, by a quarter of a century.

The Cannons have been outstandingly loyal both to the lifeboat service and to the town itself. Cruel circumstances have sometimes uprooted the Cannons and other established families, but they mostly returned to Ramsgate. Twice this century, the local fishing industry plunged into steep decline – once just before the outbreak of the First World War, and again in the 1930s, when men were driven to seek a living elsewhere. They settled in places as far away as Scotland and South Wales. Ron Cannon's father, for instance, was born in Aberdeen, but returned home within six months.

At one time in the long distant past, the fishermen of Ramsgate went in numbers and under sail to the Humber at one extreme and Penzance at the other in the search for fish. Sadly, today, only a tiny handful of small longshore boats survive, working up to four or five miles from the coast for herring, lobster and whelks.

Naturally, Ron's father joined the lifeboat and became the mechanic. Ron says there was a 'sort of sidestep' with his grandfather but his great-uncle served so the family continuity wasn't broken. Now both his sons, teenager Paul, and his elder brother, Ian, are in the present crew.

Happily, there have been no recorded disasters in the long and distinguished history of the Ramsgate boat, but young Ian Cannon once had a very narrow escape indeed, almost becoming another victim of the lethal Goodwins.

With his father in command, the Ramsgate boat had been called out in the early hours of the morning when the *Caroline* pirate radio ship broke her anchor cable and went aground on the Goodwins during turbulent seas caused by a northeasterly blowing up to force nine for two days. The cox explained what happened next.

'It took an hour to reach her, and we were instructed to stand by because a tug was coming from Dover to tow her off the sands. But after a while the *Caroline* began to roll very badly, banging on the bottom, and because she had those tall, heavy radio masts it was thought she would capsize. So the six people on board signalled that they wished to abandon ship. We were called in to take them off. Now since the *Caroline* drew sixteen feet of water and the lifeboat only just over four, we imagined there would be no risk of us going aground ourselves. What we didn't realise was that along this particular part of the Goodwins the sand is very steep – like a cliff face. The *Caroline* wasn't sitting on the sands at all. She was being slammed against the side of the sand cliff. As we came round the stern of the *Caroline*, there in front of us was virtually dry sand. I tried to avoid it by going full astern on the engines but there was so much swell running that the lifeboat was picked up like a surfboard and deposited on top of it.

'We were there for nearly twenty minutes trying to get off, for most of the time completely engulfed in water. That's when my son, Ian, who was only just seventeen at the time, almost became a casualty. He was washed over the side, but fortunately was attached to the boat by a lifeline on his jacket and his crewmates hauled him safely back in. At the time I was so engrossed with the job of refloating the boat that I didn't even know he had gone. It wasn't until we were on our way home that one of the crew told me about it.

'After we had extricated ourselves, we were standing by again, wondering what we could do next when a Sea King helicopter arrived and winched the people off the *Caroline*.'

As it happens, that was a typical conclusion to the majority of lifeboat services – long hours in hazardous conditions with nothing to show for it at the end. Only the dramatic rescues or the disasters make the headlines in the newspapers. Ron Cannon is a considered man, very eloquent about the tedious side of lifeboat service and has thought deeply about the special responsibilities of a coxswain when the adrenalin isn't running.

'Yes, you don't hear about the other side of serving in the lifeboat, when we are out searching for hour after hour, often fruitlessly. Sometimes we have to go through the night in bad weather and that's when a cox's job is really difficult, trying to keep the crew as alert as possible when there is nothing to see and nothing to do but watch and wait.

'You see, if you are searching for a casualty or someone reported missing, the place for the crew to be is on deck. It's no good being down below where it's comfortable. So everyone gets cold, wet and tired and quite often thrown around. I find that after about two hours of this men can get fed up, lose concentration and forget just what they are out there for. What I try to do in situations like that is take an extra one or two crew members so that men on deck can be relieved occasionally and go under cover.'

Ron Cannon joined the Ramsgate lifeboat when he was eighteen, more than thirty years ago. He took command on a full-time basis nineteen years ago. He still spends a limited amount of time running the small business servicing ships coming into the harbour, which was a necessary aid to making ends meet when the RNLI paid meagre wages. During his time, he has overseen the saving of many hundreds of lives, dealing with collisions at sea, ships on fire, yachts sinking and aground, all manner of sea dramas. And he holds the silver medal.

The way he earned that honour is related in a typically modest and understated way, almost as though it were just another rather hard day at the office. He makes the incident sound as if it would be infinitely preferable to patrolling endlessly and pointlessly in empty seas.

'Everything went to plan that time. It was over fairly quickly, too. The weather was extreme, though – hurricane force in fact. It started on Boxing Day in the late eighties when I was at a friend's house and heard the wind howling down the chimney. So I went down to the harbour to check that the lifeboat, which is kept afloat, was all right – and heard that a French trawler with seven crew was trying to make its way into the harbour. A communication crisis had developed. The trouble was they had built a breakwater since the French skipper had last been in Ramsgate and as he attempted to work things out the wind and tide took him to the south. He ended up aground in Pegwell Bay to the southwest of Ramsgate and put out a Mayday. His engine also packed in.

'We found him without too much difficulty, came alongside and I put two of my crew on board to overcome the language problem. Then we got a towrope aboard, the engine restarted and we helped to get her off and back into Ramsgate harbour.

Just like that. Nothing to it!

18

'Caister Men Never Turn Back' ... and Never Take No for an Answer

There are several legends and famous quotations associated with the RNLI, but none pulls at the emotions more than the tale of James Haylett, who endured the horror of watching his two sons die when the Caister lifeboat was swamped and overturned on the beach in 1901, with the loss of nine lives.

Old James had been cox of the Caister boat in his day, and at the inquest the coroner asked him why, given the seas were so bad, had the lifeboat not turned back. His proud reply has echoed down the years: 'Caister men never turn back.'

Nor, very clearly, do they take no for an answer. In 1969 the RNLI decreed that the responsibilities of the Caister boat could be absorbed by the Great Yarmouth and Gorleston boat only four miles up the coast. So, after an illustrious record stretching back 112 years (more, if you count the years they had a rescue boat before the RNLI arrived) on 19 October that year the Institution's Caister boat sailed away from the historic beach for the last time. The local reaction was predictably explosive – after all, didn't their boat hold the record for saving more lives than any other lifeboat station? A staggering total of 1,814 people, saved from the clutches of the sea by the men who never turn back.

Shortly after that bitter day, a public meeting was called and the Caister Volunteer Rescue Service was founded, money raised to form a limited company so it could become a Registered Charity and avoid any problem with the tax inspector.

Come the hour, come the man . . . A personality burst forth from the Caister crisis, who swiftly became the symbol of the spirit of this remarkable community, a true heir of James Haylett: Skipper Jack – as he is known to a wide public.

Jack Woodhouse had been the mechanic of the Caister lifeboat and he immediately took charge of the situation. On the very day the RNLI removed the boat, he replaced it in the boathouse with one of his own – a sixteen-foot fibreglass open fishing boat with a twenty-horsepower outboard engine. When a director of the RNLI, an admiral no less, asked Jack how he proposed to keep an independent lifeboat going, he replied: 'We'll have to tell 'em a good yarn and get people to give money.' And so he did, with astonishing success.

Skipper Jack is a man who has the distinction of launching a lifeboat under enemy fire, which was repeated when the boat returned.

'It was the end of 1941 when a plane had been reported on fire over the sea. It was German, although we didn't know it at the time. When we got on the beach a bomb dropped, knocking down a row of cottages and nearly blowing the lifeboat off its carriage. The second cox lived in one of those houses, but nobody was killed. When we arrived back on the beach another German plane flew just above us and we all ran for it as the bombs fell. One exploded right alongside the boat and it was damaged by the shrapnel.'

In 1970 the children of the Caister Secondary Modern School raised the cash for an inflatable boat and engine, to supplement Skipper Jack's fishing boat, and the men of Caister set about energetically saving lives – several, in fact, despite the limitations.

In 1973, Skipper Jack and his team heard that an ex-RNLI boat, which had latterly been used as a fishing boat, was being offered for sale in North Norfolk. It was a beach-launched boat of the Liverpool class, just like the one they used to have. They only had enough money to put down a deposit so, as the vessel was swiftly brought back to lifeboat standards, Skipper Jack went hunting for money and practical help. A local contractor loaned a tractor powerful enough to launch their proud new acquisition until one could be afforded. They paid off the boat, which cost £4,300, and found a suitable tractor for £3,850. Since they couldn't fly the RNLI flag, they designed one of their own, bearing the cross of St George like the Institution's but substituting the RNLI symbol with the Caister emblem of a ship's wheel.

When the refurbished boat was ready for a naming ceremony, it was decided that the privilege of choosing a name should go to the biggest donor, which led to a lady called Shirley Jean Adye, wife of that generous person, clutching the champagne bottle. But she had no idea that the Caister boat would bear her name until she broke the bottle over the bow – an indication of the style in which the independent lifeboatmen of Caister go about their business. They also possessed the imagination to match, as future events proved.

A particularly proud moment for the Caister men came in January 1978, when one of the wildest storms in living memory engulfed the coast of East Anglia. A Greek ship put out a Mayday call, giving its position as one and a half miles southeast of Lowestoft, and two RNLI boats were launched to its aid – Lowestoft, and the Great Yarmouth and Gorleston (under the command of Richard Hawkins, twin brother of the Dover cox). The height of the waves made radar searching impossible, the wind so powerful that parachute flares were unable to gain height and were hurled uselessly to one side. In the middle of this chaos, Richard Hawkins' lifeboat began to falter. First one engine stopped, and then the other. The Lowestoft boat had to abandon the search and go to the aid of its sister vessel. This created some alarm at the search headquarters situated at Gorleston, because all the other RNLI boats in the area were unable to launch because of storm damage. There was only one option left: the Caister lifeboat!

The phone rang at 2 a.m. in the home of Caister coxswain, 'Mabbey' Brown. He raced to set off the maroons, and standing among the storm wreckage around the boathouse door, asked his crew if they were prepared to go. They all agreed immediately. No way would they pass up this unexpected opportunity to prove a point to the RNLI, despite the obvious risks.

It took them almost two hours of huge effort to get the *Shirley Jean Adye* into the water. They were obliged to haul it for nearly two miles along the shore, stopping many times to try a likely place and being hurled back, until they finally got her away. And then they had the enormous pleasure and pride of calling up the search centre with a gleeful message: 'Hello, Gorleston coastguards . . . Caister lifeboat on its way to the search area!'

The Great Yarmouth and Gorleston boat had managed to get its engines going by this time, and three lifeboats swept the search area together. Althogh they were separated by only a hundred yards or so, the storm was so violent that visual contact was impossible. The Caister boat located a ship's upturned lifeboat, but on righting it found no one underneath, and then spotted a man in the water wearing a life jacket and pulled him aboard, but he was dead. The helicopter then spotted the upturned hull of the large vessel and more bodies were found. But no survivors.

In 1987, the realisation dawned that the *Shirley Jean Adye* had become a very old lady indeed. She had been launched in 1952 and her speed was only around eight knots. So the Caister Lifeboat Appeal was launched, with a target of half a million pounds, no less. Modern lifeboats are very expensive.

The appeal committee, chaired by Harry Barker, was energetically supported by John Cannell. He is a member of a crew (none of whom is paid) which recently had a remarkable cross section of backgrounds. Although they all have been associated with boats in one way or another, there was only one fisherman among them. There are plumbers, a teddy bear salesman, a school janitor, a retired window cleaner, an auxiliary coastguard, a flower salesman . . . and the Civic Head of the Borough of Great Yarmouth, of which Caister is a part. That is John Cannell.

He came up with a novel idea. Great Yarmouth has a racecourse, so a copy of the *Racehorse Owners' Handbook*, which lists names alphabetically, was acquired, and a letter seeking the donations sent to everyone from A to D. John Cannell recalls the effect.

'Over 160 letters were sent, and for a while we didn't get a single reply. Then the first one came – with £1,000. Next, Peter Cadbury, the chocolate millionaire, sent a cheque for £5,000 because of his association with Great Yarmouth. He had been born there, although I wasn't aware of that when we sent the letter. When Skipper Jack heard about this, he told us that in 1915 his father spotted a German Zeppelin approaching Great Yarmouth, informed the military and a plane was sent up to shoot it down. The pilot was Peter Cadbury's father, who was stationed at the local airfield at the time. The Skipper even produced a press cutting of the time which described the event, and he sent it off to Peter. He came to spend a day with us as a result, by which time I had found the grave of his grandfather and the place where he was born. Ever since then he has been a very good friend of the Caister lifeboat.

'Then we approached Bernard Matthews, the Norfolk turkey producer of "Bootiful" fame. He made a major donation, and persuaded a lot of his friends to follow suit. Prince Charles gave his support, and came to inspect the station. He took a trip on the old boat and we presented him with a box of Caister kippers.'

John and his team then targeted the media and the world of show business – many stars play Great Yarmouth in the season. Newspapers took up the story, Anglia TV produced a documentary entitled *Keep the Boat Afloat*, and the money began to flow in.

Skipper Jack, although approaching his eighties, also got to work in brilliant style. He generated the kind of nationwide publicity that most fundraisers can only dream about. The first Terry Wogan show he did brought in £30,000. There was a memorable moment on the programme when Terry Wogan discovered that Skipper Jack couldn't swim, and asked him what he would do if ever he fell overboard.

'That'd be the time to learn, wouldn't it!' replied Skipper Jack.

Then Michael Aspel turned up with a red book bearing the Skipper's name and the enormous *This Is Your Life* audience got the Caister message. Meanwhile, the Skipper and the committee turned their attention to other famous personalities. An opportunity arrived one day when Mike Reid got his Jaguar bogged down in the sand on Caister beach. Skipper Jack hauled him out with his tractor. Mike launched his speedboat and promptly got that stuck on a sandbank. Later, it sprung a leak when his wife, sister-in-law and children, but not he, were on board. The Caister boat came to the rescue once again. Another handsome contribution.

In 1987, Bobby Davro and Russ Abbot staged a show which raised a substantial sum, and Freddie Starr and The Grumbleweeds followed with another the year after. Then it was Jim Davidson's turn. John Cannell met him – 'Just casually, you know!' – when he was starring in a Great Yarmouth summer show.

'What a character he is! I asked him to do a charity event for us but he said he didn't do them. Then he asked where the Caister boys had a drink and later turned up at the Never Turn Back, the local pub named after that historic declaration, and the session carried on in his dressing room after we had seen his show. He then announced that he would have to do something for us. The following Sunday lunchtime he turned up at the pub again with half a dozen of his friends from the theatre band, completely unannounced, set up outside and began giving a concert with himself on the drums. Twice he did that. Some people complained to the police about the noise. Afterwards he decided to do a midnight show and packed out the theatre, all money going to us – £10,000. Cheques for as much as £5,000 arrive at the pub – he never sends them to the lifeboat station – and in 1991 he bought us an inshore lifeboat which, naturally, was named after him. Altogether up to now, Jim Davidson has been responsible for putting £50,000 into our funds. He has a very strong affinity with us, goes around to Skipper Jack's house like he was one of the boys and we all have a healthy respect for him – and not just because of the money. He is a very good seaman, with a boat of his own, and a deep knowledge of the sea.'

In between hobnobbing with celebrities and millionaires, the Caister men were also going about the business of attending to those in peril on the sea. There were some spectacular episodes. One of them followed to the letter that clarion call, 'Caister men never turn back.'

On 9 December 1993, they launched into the teeth of another lethal gale in response to a Mayday from a Dutch fishing boat, which had lost a man overboard – some forty miles off the coast. The Caister boat, with cox Richard Thurlow at the helm, ploughed through waves reaching to thirty feet. Because the wind, which was bending their aerials forward, was on the stern, they were surfing along at a speed of twenty-six knots. On the way all their instruments bar the compass and direction finder were put out of action by the violence of the storm. Heading for the same casualty was the Great Yarmouth and Gorleston boat, which was to run into serious trouble. When they had made fifteen miles, coastguard control radioed the Caister boat, saying that the conditions out there were very bad, a Royal Naval destroyer, HMS *Nottingham*, had arrived on the scene and would it not be prudent to turn back?

With no little pride, Richard Thurlow gave the traditional Caister reply: 'We are quite happy to keep going!'

'Immediately I said that, the RNLI boat also said they would press on, too. Unfortunately, they had a really bad time. I understand they were knocked on to their beam ends twice at around eight miles out, and then almost capsized. Both engines stopped, and the crew could only get one started again, so they signalled that they reluctantly had to turn back. We managed to reach the search area where they calculated the man may have drifted, and kept going until 5 a.m. In case of a capsize I split the crew of nine, keeping four on deck and sending five down below, which would put us in a better position if the worst happened.'

In those conditions, the outcome was inevitable, and at 5 a.m. the captain of the destroyer, Commander Ian Moncrieff, in consultation with the rescue control, signalled a termination of the search because there was no further hope of the poor fisherman surviving. Hypothermia would have surely claimed him by then, even if he hadn't drowned.

A few days later, Commander Moncrieff, who also happened to be an RNLI shoreline member for years (along with his wife), dispatched a letter to the director of the RNLI, which contained a firm indication that he thought the Caister crew deserved an award from the Institution. He was obviously under the impression they were RNLI men. In it he declared:

> It was clear the [Caister] lifeboat was working at the very limits of, if not beyond, its operating envelope, then the coxswain remained a cheerful voice on VHF, with an incredible sense of determination and professionalism towards the search. Indeed, my people were simply amazed as to how this small craft had managed to get on the scene . . . he regularly disappeared among the high waves and turning across the sea must have been particulary dangerous . . . all who witnessed, including some army personnel, the lifeboat's work and fortitude were full of admiration for the courage the crew displayed . . . throughout the incident your people showed incredible bravery and stamina . . . an extraordinary feat of seamanship.
>
> Whether or not your organisation chooses to recognise the Caister team for some appropriate form of award is within your gift, and I never did get the coxswain's name; but I would be grateful if you would pass on the admiration and respect from all in HMS *Nottingham*. If nothing else, you may find a few more coins in the lifeboat slot next time one of my crew goes past the collecting box.

Richard Thurlow and his crew received a copy of the letter . . . but nothing else. Curiously enough, a Caister lifeboatman did get an award on the very day the crew were winning the Commander's admiration. Skipper Jack Woodhouse went to London to receive the MBE. In defence of the management of the RNLI, the Caister men were honoured in 1986 with an official RNLI vellum award – the next best thing to a bronze – for rescuing eight men from a rig supply vessel, *Seaforth Conqueror*. And there is one honour granted to every member of the lifeboat crew – no doubt due to the influence of crewman John Cannell. They automatically become freemen of the Borough of Great Yarmouth.

By 1991, the fund had reached its target and they went shopping for a boat. A marine company in Rye was marketing a thirty-eight-foot Brede lifeboat, hoping to break into the RNLI market, but the design was turned down. Nevertheless, after much consideration, the Caister management concluded it was just right for their purpose and bought one. Various companies gave equipment and did electrical and other work, to the value of £100,000 – all for free.

On 19 June 1991, the new boat was named and dedicated in the presence of Her Royal Highness Princess Alexandra, an occasion of enormous triumph, proving that nothing will stop the men of Caister – neither personal disaster, hurricanes, rejection by their parent body, nor even German bombs.

It remains the only lifeboat of its kind in Britain and was named the *Bernard Matthews*, in honour of the prime benefactor.

The Caister roll of honour includes many recent notable exploits, performed with the usual courage and determination that comes into the category of sheer obstinacy, the very hallmark of the men of Caister. Just one of those that stands out occurred when a forty-seven-foot boat with a family on board encountered engine trouble in the middle of the night, three miles east of Caister. They were on their way to Ipswich to pick up stores before proceeding to Portugal. The coastguard asked Richard Thurlow to summon the crew as quickly as possible because of the severe danger the yacht was facing.

'At Caister we have a notorious sandbank to the east which runs for ten miles and I knew if they were on this and didn't get help quickly it would be their grave. The launch had to be so quick that we didn't have time to load the portable water pump. We hadn't been afloat very long before they were putting life jackets on in the casualty, ready to abandon ship, so we ran across the sandbank in heavy surf, banging all the way since it was only a metre of water beneath us. At first, we couldn't see them and had to radio them to fire a distress flare. They were in a severe state of shock when we found them – a man, a woman, two children aged eight and six and two dogs. We went in but they wouldn't jump so the next time I brought her alongside John Cannell jumped aboard – he has done that before, rather specialises in it. I ran in again and John passed over one sobbing child, backed off and repeated the manoeuvre. The woman, who was also crying, refused to jump, so John just picked her up and literally threw her across to us which made the dogs aggressive – and they were both Alsatians! Eventually we got the entire family aboard and down in the survivors' cabin, dogs included. The women and children promptly went to sleep!

'Billy Read, the second cox, joined John on the yacht, attached a towline and after twenty minutes we had wriggled it off the sandbank. Then John discovered that she was taking in water rather badly. The engines were submerged. And we had left our portable pump behind.

'The RNLI inshore boat from Gorleston arrived to help and kindly went back to Caister to pick up the pump, but it wouldn't work properly. So we decided we should make a run for it, towing as hard as we could, reasoning that if we kept the water at the stern away from the bulkhead we had a chance of saving her. We couldn't let the damned thing sink in deep water because it was their home – everything they had. Another pump was called for, and arrived with the Gorleston big boat just in time. Another ten minutes and we would have lost it. The fire brigade was waiting in the harbour with a big pump, but as soon as they stopped it went to the bottom. At least it wasn't lost. They refloated it and eventually went on their way again.'

Sadly, tragedy returned once again to that Caister beach, less than two months after the joyous christening of their brand-new boat. On 1 September 1991, the cox, Benny Read, came to the lifeboat house to organise a launch. It was blowing hard as he prepared the maroon, which turned out to be faulty. When he lit the fuse there was immediate ignition and he didn't have time to move back. It hit him full in the chest and killed him. Skipper Jack was the first on the scene. Unfortunately, his wife was listening on the radio as a coastguard summoned a helicopter ambulance.

Later on, when the press came down, Skipper Jack was asked if this meant the Caister station would close down. He rose superbly to the occasion once again.

'Did they close down the Royal Navy when Nelson was killed?'

19

The Greatest Lifeboatman of Them All

A few miles further north along the Norfolk coast from Caister stands the very attractive Victorian seaside town of Cromer, home of the man who is universally acknowledged to be the greatest lifeboatman of all time, Henry Blogg.

There have been hundreds of astonishing feats of courage and determination by RNLI men during the last 200 years, but those achieved by Henry Blogg were practically superhuman. He was the cox of the Cromer boat from 1909 until 1948, supervised the saving of 873 lives and won an unprecedented, probably never-to-be-equalled three gold medals and four silver. His exploits in the primitive open boats of his day made him a media legend, standing shoulder to shoulder with the contemporary show business and sporting heroes in the affection of the general public. He must have done more for the reputation – not to mention the funds – of the RNLI than any single person since Grace Darling. Henry provided for many thousands of people the most thrilling theatre of their lives, since several of his rescues were carried out in full view of the coast. Henry could pull bigger audiences than the Edwardian vaudeville stars like Harry Lauder. Holidaymakers, drawn by the noise of the maroons, would pack the Cromer promenade, spellbound by the sight of Henry and his crew launching into tumultuous seas, often thrown back on to the beach, but never giving up. Then, witnessing a hazardous rescue in the distance (once to a ship blown in half by a mine) with the vulnerable lifeboat being pitched and tossed around the stricken vessel as it snatched people from certain death, would cheer themselves hoarse as Henry returned with the survivors. Journalists and newsreel crews were continually scrambling for Cromer.

The genealogy of the present cox of the Cromer lifeboat demonstrates yet again the family continuity in so many lifeboat communities. As a boy, Richard Davies knew the immortal Henry very well. He was his great-uncle. Richard's great-grandmother was Henry's mother. A rather delicate matter is involved here. It seemed that Helen Blogg was not married when she gave birth to Henry in 1876. She later married John Davies, Richard's great-grandfather, who willingly took care of Henry and brought him up, as well as fathering two sons and two daughters of his own. Apparently, the identity of Henry's real father was not revealed.

There are three or four fishing families in Cromer with proud records of lifeboat service stretching back to the beginning of the nineteenth century, but two have united in what can only be described as an heroic dynasty, the Davieses and the Harrisons.

The Harrisons were flourishing in Cromer when the first lifeboat arrived in 1804, the year before Trafalgar (and very likely had a sibling or two serving under Nelson). Richard's ancestor, John James Davies, was a cattle drover from Wales who regularly walked all the way to Cromer with a herd of cattle for sale, which meant that the exporting of live British meat may have been going on for more than two and a half centuries. On one visit John James met Phoebe Harrison, and in 1824 married her and settled in Cromer. From then on the two families have generated an endless supply of coxswains and crewmen for the lifeboat.

Today, the management of the Cromer boat is conducted under the eagle gaze of two retired coxswains, both in their eighties. Lewis 'Tuner' Harrison and Henry 'Shrimp' Davies. Both are related to the cox, Richard Davies. The intricate web of relationships between these two families, compounded by nicknames, can leave the innocent enquirer quite dizzy. Tuner received his nickname because of his habit as a boy of singing first thing in the morning. Shrimp had the honour of being so dubbed by Henry Blogg himself. He was so tiny when he was born that on first sight Henry, his uncle and namesake, declared that he looked more like a shrimp than a baby.

Shrimp is also very proud of the fact that a certain lady whom he describes as 'probably the greatest in the land' knows and refers to him by his nickname – Her Majesty, Queen Elizabeth, The Queen Mother.

'I went to give a talk to the Women's Institute at Sandringham, which is only forty miles from Cromer, when the Queen Mother was President. When I arrived she sat down with me and had a chat and then introduced me as Shrimp Davies, cox of the Cromer lifeboat. She seemed very pleased with my talk and asked me if I would go and help judge the homemade jam and wine. But I wasn't allowed to taste. She told me you could test a jar of jam by turning it upside down, and if it hung there you knew it was all right.

'So I said: "Ma'am – how do you guess how good the wine is without trying it? You must taste it."

'But she said: "No, I'm afraid not," and went about making notes as to colour and clarity. I asked her if she was looking for anything in particular, and she said she was – wheat and potato wine. She declared that if there was a bottle of that on the table she would give it first prize, no matter what it looked like, because half a glass of that was enough to knock the top of your head off – her very words.

'Then she went on to tell me a story about her childhood, when she would go around the family estate with her father, he on his horse and she on her pony. They would call regularly at a certain cottage, and her father would be met by a woman and be taken inside. As she grew up, the future Queen of England said she really began to wonder what was going on until, when she was around sixteen or seventeen, the lady came to the door of the cottage and said to her father: "Sir, I think she's old enough now, don't you?" He agreed that this was probably true, and the Queen Mother discovered that he had been calling for a drop of wheat and potato wine.

'The Queen Mother told me that she herself called at the cottage many times after that. And ever since she told me about it I have been trying to find a bottle myself to send to her as a birthday present.'

Both Shrimp Davies and Tuner Harrison were born into this fishing community when the twentieth century was still young, and large families were commonplace. Since it was traditional to repeat the same name down the male line, nicknames were widespread. For instance, Tuner's father was known as 'Tater' Harrison, one brother was 'Yakker' because he stuttered and the other, more obscurely, became 'Kelly', after the doll that always rolls back up after being knocked down.

When he left school at the age of fourteen, Tuner vainly tried to avoid following the family tradition.

'I wanted to be a mechanic, but Father took me to sea with him. In those days you did as you were told and no arguments. Same with the lifeboat – you didn't volunteer, you were expected to join when you aged seventeen. My father was the cox, so the first loud noises I heard as a child were the maroons going off and my father and elder brothers shouting as they ran to launch the lifeboat.'

Richard Davies was another who nursed ambitions outside fishing, and serving in the lifeboat.

'I had this love for animals and wanted to go and work on a farm because every time I went to sea I was ill. But in my final school year, the old man pulled me out at Easter instead of the end of the summer term because Easter was the start of the crabbing season. I was sick every day. It went on for two years. I can remember saying to my father that I wanted to die, and he replied with a few choice words. "Die when you are home," he said. You were more likely to get a clip around the earhole than sympathy. But we all had to go through it – Grandfather was the same – and I got over it in the end.

'Now my boy, John James, is just the opposite. I took him to sea when he was three years old and he loved it. Couldn't keep him out of the boat.'

Naturally, John James Davies is a member of the Cromer lifeboat crew, and together with his father runs three fishing boats and a very popular fish retail shop in the centre of Cromer. They hunt crabs, herring, cod – and that traditional favourite with most tourists and all cockneys – whelks. However, the biggest market for whelks today is Japan.

The family record of service with the RNLI must be unique. It began in 1804 with Richard's great-great-grandfather, and carried on in an unbroken line through five generations to his son, every one of them called John James Davies, except Richard. Including Great-uncle Henry's three golds and four silvers, they have harvested eighty-two medals and awards between them up to now. Great-grandfather Davies also won the Royal Humane Society's coveted medal.

Richard recalls one family legend which amply demonstrates

how hard and uncompromising it was necessary to be to survive and succeed in Cromer long ago. One of the John Jameses was nicknamed 'Cropper'. He came by that name one day when his daughter, who had long hair, came home crying and sporting a black eye. She had come off worse in an argument with another girl, who had pulled her about by her hair. So her father got some scissors, cropped all her hair off and ordered her to go back and fight!

The prolific male line of the Davies family almost came to an abrupt end in 1941 when a twenty-foot-high wave burst over Cromer lifeboat. Richard understands that of the twelve crew, all but two were members of the Davies family. Henry Blogg was there, as well as Shrimp Davies, with his father, grandfather and younger brother, plus Richard's grandfather, his brother and their sons.

Six men were washed overboard by that wave. If the lifeboat had capsized and thrown the lot out, that would have been the Davies family name wiped out, because it wasn't a self-righter. There would have been no hope for any of them. But the six who clung on managed to drag the others back on board.

Since he was one who ended up in the sea, Shrimp recalls the incident in clear detail.

'We were trying to get alongside a ship called the *English Trader*, when the lifeboat went on its beam ends. There were no lifelines in those days. Anyway, the six who stayed in the boat fished us out and we returned to complete the job in the early hours of the next morning when conditions were calmer. Unfortunately, our signalman, Walter Allen, member of another old Cromer family, didn't survive. He was still alive when pulled out of the sea but died later. It transpired he had a heart condition, but didn't tell anyone. He was like that. First-class man, was Walter.'

Shrimp was awarded a bronze for his courage on that mission.

It was during Shrimp's tenure in command of the boat that Richard Davies had a remarkably early introduction to the Cromer boat, despite his distaste for the sea.

'I was about twelve at the time, and was with my cousin, Billy Davies, who was only eight, when the maroons were put up. Father asked if we wanted to go, and before the rest of the crew arrived smuggled us aboard and hid us in the rope locker. After the boat was launched he told us we could come out. Shrimp was annoyed at first, wanted to know what the hell we were doing there, but Dad just laughed. Billy and I watched as the lifeboat came alongside this ship and an injured man was lowered down in a stretcher. Then we went to school. Like me, Billy became a crew member when he was old enough.'

In keeping with family tradition, Richard, now approaching his fifties, added a bronze to that amazing collection in 1993 when he coxed the lifeboat to a difficult rescue of a yacht in distress in dangerous shoal waters. Characteristically, he prefers to talk about his admiration for another award winner, who was not a typical crew member.

'It happened in 1973 when I was a crewman. Gas bottles exploded on a trawler, killing one man, injuring another and wrecking the steering gear. So we took our doctor, poor devil! Dr Paul Barclay came straight from his surgery, stepped into an open boat, and sailed directly into a good gale of wind. It was really rough, and he was bad. I can see him now hanging over the side, soaking wet. He was getting on a bit at the time too, but when I jumped to get on the trawler and turned around to see where he was, I found him right behind me.

'Well, one man had an arm blown off and the back of his head had gone, too. The skipper was covered in splinters from the door of his cabin, and the mate was in shock. But that doctor did such a good job, ill as he was. I stayed with him all the time until the helicopter took him and the skipper off as the trawler was towed back.

'Dr Barclay was awarded the bronze medal. I was very pleased for him – he really earned it.'

Incidentally, Richard Davies, who has the rare distinction in Cromer of not possessing a nickname, retains his love of animals. He has two dogs, a tank full of tropical fish and a parrot at home, and around six racing greyhounds in training kennels.

20

Dylan Thomas and the Buoy Boy

The small and somewhat remote Welsh sea village of Newquay perches prettily on the Cardiganshire coast and is historically notable for at least two reasons: Dylan Thomas lived there for a while, and the community hung on to a sail and manpowered lifeboat until 1948, the last survivor of that legendary breed graced by figures of the past such as Henry Blogg. Engines were first used in lifeboats as early as 1889 – steam, as it happens, which must have made swift launches a problem – but they didn't like to rush things in Newquay.

It is a highly visual place, full of colourful and slightly eccentric characters. The rather outrageous man generally regarded as one of the finest British poets of the century must have felt at home there. The bar at the Black Lion where he was wont to slake his famously prodigious thirst is named in his honour, hung with suitable mementos and stacked with his volumes. The 'miscellaneous retired sea captains' who 'emerged . . . from deeper waves than ever tossed their boats', from *Quite Early One Morning*, are thought to be a reference to the regulars of the Black Lion and there are claims that he began work on *Under Milk Wood* during the sixteen months he spent in Newquay.

This reflected fame does not impress many locals, particularly one leading resident, Dennis Leworthy, the honorary secretary of the Newquay lifeboat, one of the few lifeboatmen around today who can claim the distinction of serving in a primitive sail and oar boat. He regards the great poet with absolute distaste.

'I knew him. I used to see him in the Black Lion, when I came home from sea, but I would not lower my dignity to drink with him. He was a damned waster, nothing more. He came here and conned everybody for drinks and other favours, and he wasn't even a real Welshman – he couldn't speak Welsh.'

It appears that more resentment was created because Dylan Thomas arrived in this somewhat close-knit community from London during wartime. Many of Newquay's young men were away fighting (and some dying) for their country, but Dylan wasn't. His Bohemian lifestyle and constant drinking with other literary figures, escaping the danger posed by the Luftwaffe in London, did not go down well with people who had sons away at sea.

Dennis Leworthy, one son of Newquay risking his neck in Far Eastern waters at the time, does admit to socialising once, somewhat unofficially, with the poet during one spell of leave.

'We gate-crashed one of his parties, held in the bungalow he rented across the bay. An army major enlivened the proceedings by firing at the ceiling with his Sten gun. We beat a hasty retreat over the cliff and down the beach before the police arrived.'

By that time, the young leading seaman was well accustomed to gunfire. The son of a deep-sea fisherman, James Leworthy, who was the first Newquay man to die in the First World War when his ship was mined off the Scottish coast, Dennis joined the Royal Navy before his sixteenth birthday and served a total of twelve years. By the time he reached eighteen he was in action against the Japanese, hauling cordite and shells for the guns of the battle-class destroyer HMS *Camperdown*, which had a crew of 300 and a remarkable turn of speed – thirty knots. That came in handy when it was dodging Japanese air attacks.

Dennis Leworthy is reluctant to talk about his war experiences, but does tell one story which has a curious mix of light and dark.

'I was a buoy boy on the *Camperdown*. That meant I had to jump on buoys to attach the ship's wire hawser when we tied up. Now buoys had a nasty habit of twisting and turning, and once when we were on the Yangtze river in China, I was sent spinning into the water. In that part of the Yangtze there was an eight-knot tide and I was quickly swept away towards the sea. They launched the liberty boat and set off in pursuit but it took over an hour before they got to me. Now I didn't exactly enjoy the swim but I was much more worried about going anywhere near a boom defence wire further down the Yangtze. The Chinese dumped unwanted female babies in the river, thousands of them, and I knew dredgers went to that boom every month to gather up the babies and take them out to sea.

'If I had have arrived there I would have died of fright.'

The buoy boy's first taste of service on the lifeboat came just before he went into the navy, when he was only fifteen – against RNLI rules, but the year was 1941 and most local men had gone to fight. He was an oarsman in the eight-man crew and it appears that his proudest moment did not, by lifeboat standards, involve anything particularly hazardous or heroic.

'A submarine being towed in very bad weather from Liverpool to Pembroke broke its line and called for assistance – someone to stand by ready to move in if it became necessary to rescue the crew until a tug could be summoned. Three lifeboats were launched – Fishguard, Aberystwyth and us, all at the same time. The other two had engines, and we went under sail – mainsail and mizzen. She was a lovely old thing, thirty-eight feet long and built in 1907. We had to winch her by hand into the boathouse, three men to a side.

'Now on that submarine job we had the furthest to go and we arrived there first!'

When it comes to the question of the courage required to go out in a lifeboat, Dennis Leworthy, now approaching seventy, is drily dismissive.

'In my day you didn't go out to be a hero. I think I went for the seven shillings and sixpence more than anything. When we went out on exercise the cox would shout, "Pull like hell," then say, "Hold water!" and offer seven and sixpence to the first man to break an oar. Ye gods, if a fifteen-year-old like me had tried to go for that, he would have been shot to the back of the boat like a bullet, and the oar over the side! I never did see anyone break an oar!'

Of course, the men of the Newquay lifeboat have known high drama and displayed courage of the highest order since their station was founded more than 150 years ago. Perhaps the most noteworthy in recent years occurred in the seventies when one of the worst storms in living memory tore from its anchorage an enormous Ministry of Defence barge, used for tracking missiles fired from Aberporth. It measured 300 feet by 125 feet and carried equipment worth at least a million pounds. About twenty men were permanently quartered on it. Even Dennis Leworthy is stirred by the memories of that night.

'Those were the most violent conditions I have ever known the boat to face. It was blowing a northwesterly up to force ten. The launch was in the early hours and we were supposed to take the crew off. But they refused. I don't know what was going through their minds – perhaps they thought someone might claim salvage.'

Throughout the night the barge fought to survive. It was stationed ten miles offshore to begin with and was being driven inexorably by the storm towards the shore and disaster. A helicopter flew anchors out to her, as big as could safely be carried, and took some of the crew off. But nothing would hold her. A minesweeper arrived to take her in tow, but apparently fouled her propeller on a wire rope. That was when the Newquay lifeboat was called out to stand by. Mechanic Mervyn Thomas was on board.

'In the end they were very, very lucky. The barge was only about half a mile offshore when an anchor finally held. They had actually cut away all the guardrails down one side of the barge, ready to push over a large crane attached to a wire rope to act as an anchor as a last resort. The crane must have been worth £100,000, but that's nothing compared to a million pounds, plus the value of the barge.'

Around the same time Mervyn Thomas took the lead in a service which earned him a bronze medal. An open motor cruiser with three men on board had broken down in a fierce ground sea created by a gale which had lasted for several days. It managed to anchor in a perilous position near some cliffs – considered too near for the big boat to approach safely – so the Newquay inshore boat, manned by three men, launched with Mervyn at the helm.

'When we arrived on the scene, two men had swum for the shore. One was lying on a rock on the beach, and the other was on top of a cliff, obviously exhausted. How on earth he managed to get up there I'll never know – desperation, I suppose. The third was still in the boat. I learned later they were all policemen.

'I made the decision to go for the man on the beach first, dropped the anchor and backed in under the cliff. But we were caught by an awkward wave which lifted us on top of a ledge. It gave us the chance to put one man ashore to grab the man and bring him aboard. As he did so, the inshore boat was washed off the ledge. We managed to grab the policeman but our crewman, Richard Phillips, was left behind and our radio aerial was broken in the process. That created a dilemma – I had one man in my boat suffering from hypothermia and various injuries, there was another one still on the cliff and the motor cruiser was starting to drag its anchor. And I had no radio. So I sent up a red flare to call out the big boat and shot off to a village in a cove about four miles down the coast to get the one we had secured into warmth and shelter.

'It all worked out well in the end. I steered through the breakers towards Richard, who swam out and grabbed a lifeline. The big boat managed to tow the cruiser to safety with the man still sitting in it, and the coastguards found the one on the cliff and organised an ambulance.'

In contrast, however, the Newquay men tell a heartbreaking story of another man who managed to save himself from a raging sea by swimming ashore. He was sailing alone from Cardigan in his yacht and vanished. The Fishguard lifeboat searched in vain for more than five hours during the night, the helicopter and the Newquay boat joined in at daybreak and his empty boat was eventually found washed ashore at Penbryn. Then they located the man.

He had made it safely to land, climbed a cliff and crawled through a field. From there he would be able to see a light in the distance. A farmhouse. Warmth and safety! What relief that wretched man must have felt at that moment. He made his way in the pitch-black towards the light, fell into a silage pit and drowned.

21

Snarling Mountains of Fury . . . And Two Lads Ready to Die For a Pint

As a geographical entity in the global sense, the Isle of Anglesey is as insignificant as a place can get. A mere speck of dust falling from the skirts of a small island off the European mainland, around twenty miles from coast to coast whichever way you measure it, and not much in between.

But there is undeniably a great deal to say about Anglesey in lifeboat terms. Before the RNLI first came into being as the National Institution for the Preservation of Life from Shipwrecks, on 4 March 1824, there were twenty-eight independent organisations dedicated to saving those in peril on the sea already operating from around the shores of these islands. Eighteen of them were situated along the coasts of Anglesey. Today there are four RNLI stations – at Holyhead, Beaumaris, Trearddur Bay and Moelfre, still an extraordinarily high number for such a small patch.

And of these, Moelfre has a truly spectacular record. It is the home of the greatest living lifeboatman, retired coxswain Dick Evans, who won two gold medals, one bronze and the Queen's Award for Gallantry. A book has been written about his career, and he was besieged by television crews when he celebrated his ninetieth birthday in 1995.

Dick has a warm and confident personality and can always be relied upon to come up with the sort of sound bites that gladden a producer's heart. His lyrical description of the sea he faced when he won his first gold in 1959 is well remembered – 'snarling mountains of fury'. Those who preceded Dick in the Moelfre boat also struck gold on a regular basis. A total of five of these very rare honours have been won in pitched battles with the sea around this tiny village over the last 170 years. The gold is the lifeboatman's VC. Only thirty-three have been awarded this century, just nine since the last war.

Oddly enough, only two days before Dick faced those menacing mountains, he and his crew had been attending the memorial service for the loss of the *Royal Charter*, which foundered close to Moelfre 100 years previously, on 25 October 1859. A service has been held every year since then at the church where those bodies that were recovered are buried. More than 400 perished on the last leg of a journey which the 2,719-ton passenger ship was making from Melbourne to Liverpool. They were just a day away from safety. Out of the total of nearly 500 passengers and crew, a mere 41 survived. The same storm, of unparalleled savagery, had swept across Britain sinking 133 ships and claiming 800 lives.

Exactly a century and two days later, Dick Evans went out in frighteningly similar circumstances to the aid of a 506-ton coaster called the *Hindlea*, which was dragging her starboard anchor in Dulas Bay off the east coast of Anglesey. The wind was gusting to 100 miles an hour plus. When the *Hindlea* was forced to a position only 200 yards away from rocks the captain gave the order to abandon ship. The Moelfre lifeboat, which had been standing by for well over an hour, moved in and rolled over on to her beam ends as a huge wave engulfed her, then threw her terrifyingly close to the *Hindlea*'s thrashing propeller.

Then the lifeboat collided heavily with the *Hindlea*, almost landing on its deck. But Dick pressed calmly on. Ten times he drove his forty-one-foot boat with consummate skill back towards the *Hindlea*, which had a crew of eight. Only twice did he fail to pick off a man. Finally he got them all!

The *Hindlea* was 100 yards away from the rocks when Dick turned triumphantly for home. It was torn in two soon afterwards.

Every man in the crew got a medal. Dick his gold, the mechanic, Evan Owens, a silver and the rest bronze.

There are two major reasons why Anglesey has such a history

of high action, as the present cox of the Moelfre lifeboat, Thomas Jones, explains.

'Our position on the approaches to Liverpool, once the biggest seaport in the world, is one. The speed and unpredictability of the weather is the other. Anglesey is different. We tend not to get seas building up over days and sometimes weeks like other places. Bad weather is often instantaneous here. We get no warning. The wind can pick up as the tide turns and go from force two to three to gale eight in ten minutes. And it can stop as quickly as it starts. It tends to catch everyone out, particularly yachtsmen, and that's the reason why this is such a busy station.'

Apparently, it can help to possess a certain status when you find yourself in trouble in your yacht off the coast of Anglesey. It seems Mayday calls from boats stricken by a sudden squall must be so commonplace that a relaxed (but always responsible) attitude may sometimes be detected. Thomas Jones knows of one curious example.

'The coastguards rather reluctantly called us out to a yacht which had been dismasted about six miles out from Moelfre. It was only blowing around a force six so they were very laid back about it at first. But the situation changed rapidly when they had further conversation on the radio with the yachtsman and found out he was Lord something or other. Then it became very urgent!

'We located him, and put one of our crewmen aboard, a big strong lad, who helped his Lordship to get the mast and rigging back in the boat and lashed down before we towed him in. But the most bizarre incident of all in my experience happened in 1994 when a pair of Irishman set off in an inflatable boat from Strangford Lough in Ulster to go to Peel, on the Isle of Man – for a pint!

'They managed to miss the Isle of Man completely and ran out of fuel. No one knew where they were but, thank God, they had a radio and were able to call up the coastguard. We were sent out to look for them. By that time it had started to blow up a bit and the forecast was not good. The coastguards became very concerned.

'They told us to steam north. We had picked up these lads on the radio and the direction finder had told us that they were ahead. But we didn't know how far. Neither did we know how big their boat was. We fired a flare and asked whether they could see it, and they replied that they could – just. So we asked them to fire a flare themselves to guide us to them, and they said they would. But we saw nothing. The mechanic called back to ask what was happening and the lad said they had tried, but the flare hadn't gone off, and what should they do with it? The mechanic told him to throw it overboard quickly – it could explode in their boat. That was done, and their second flare did work. But it only peeped over the horizon for a second. We still couldn't tell how far away they were, but we knew we were going the right way. They had no lights, but we put all our searchlights on and they eventually saw us.

'Then this thing appeared out of the gloom. It was an inflatable, only sixteen feet long. Two lads in their twenties were sitting in it dressed in their going out gear – no oilskins or proper clothing of any kind, just sweaters and jeans. They were very happy to see us, I can tell you – and very cold. I don't think they would have lasted much longer. They hadn't a clue where they were or where we were from. It turned out they hadn't even heard of Anglesey, let alone Moelfre. We towed them back in and gave them a tot of whisky. Our head launcher put them up for the night and gave them breakfast.

'First thing they asked next morning was the quickest way back to Ireland. All the lads chorused: "On the ferry!" But they decided to sail back, taking extra fuel this time, and agreeing to go by the Isle of Man. It is seventy-three miles from Moelfre to Strangford Lough.

'They found the Isle of Man this time, but lost their way again between there and Ireland. The Newcastle, County Down, lifeboat had to be called out. Two lifeboat launches – and all for the want of a pint!'

22

Across the Sea to Ireland – and Deadly Dublin Bay

That stretch of water between the Anglesey port of Holyhead and the Republic of Ireland has long been one of the most well-worn sea paths in Europe, and is as traditionally troublesome as the politics of Ireland itself. But even the fearsome reputation of the Irish Sea was once transcended by that of one of its gateways: Dublin Bay.

Two hundred years ago, Captain Malcolm, George III's Yacht-master, and Commander of the Royal Yacht *William and Mary*, wrote:

> The Bay of Dublin has perhaps been more fatal to ships and seamen than any in the world. A ship once caught in it in a gale of wind from east-northeast to south-southeast must ride at her anchors or go on shore, and from the nature of that shore, the whole of the crews almost invariably perished.

And that opinion led to the formation of the very first lifeboat service, according to Dr John de Courcy, the president of the Dun Laoghaire Branch, who in May 1995 was installed as an honorary life governor of the RNLI, which is the highest honour the Institution can confer on honorary members. The Irish section of the lifeboat service, incidentally, did not split from the mother organisation as the Republic of Ireland was born, wisely preferring to distance the business of saving lives from the endless strife and bitterness of Anglo-Irish relations. Yet it seems it was born out of a political act, as Dr de Courcy explained.

'When the old Irish Parliament was dissolved by the Act of Union in 1801, the last thing it did was to ask the Dublin Port Authority to look into the possibility of setting up a lifeboat service. I think we were the first. Not the first station by a long way, but the first service. Six stations were set up, and they were very badly needed.

'However, it may not have been just the gales that caused so much havoc in Dublin Bay. In the very same year that the lifeboat stations were opened, Captain Bligh, no less, the Master of the *Bounty*, came to chart the bay. The Royal Dublin Society still has his report in its archives and it is fascinating to read. Bligh declared that the terrible reputation of Dublin Bay was largely due to the meanness of shipowners, who would not pay for proper anchors and sufficient cable to prevent ships being dragged ashore by those wicked easterlies.

'It was another tragic example of meanness which led to the RNLI taking over our lifeboat station in 1862. The cox of the Dun Laoghaire lifeboat then was also the harbour master, William Hutchison. He had repeatedly told the port authorities that his boat was not serviceable. When a dreadful storm arose in February 1861, he refused to launch the lifeboat but went instead to Captain John McNeill Boyd, Commander of the Royal Naval guardship, *Ajax*, and asked for help. Together with their men, the two of them went on the pier to try and rescue the crews of two schooners which had been driven up against it. Huge seas were coming across the harbour and Captain McNeill – a distinguished Crimean veteran who had written the last battle manual for sailing warships – was swept to his death along with six of his men. Hutchison managed to hang on to something and survived.

'Thirty ships were lost in that storm, and there was such a scandal in the press, who wanted to know where the lifeboat had been. Hutchison explained why he declined to launch it. He said he wasn't going to be responsible for sending fifteen men to certain death. So the RNLI was asked to take over. Hutchison proved his bravery during a similar storm in 1829, and won the Institution's gold medal.'

Like so many lifeboat stations of long standing, Dun Laoghaire has suffered its share of disaster. On Christmas Eve 1895, the entire crew was wiped out. And it speaks much for the fearless

Thirty men to each rope – a pre-war launch of the St Ives lifeboat

. . . and a dash to launch in more recent times.

Above left: John Stevens – his 'angels' told him not to go. (*Courtesy of Yorkshire TV*)

Above right: Eric Ward, artist and coxswain, at the helm of the St Ives lifeboat. (*Photo by Phil Monckton*)

Below: William Freeman – sole survivor of the 1939 St Ives lifeboat disaster. (*Courtesy of Yorkshire TV*)

Dan Paynter, Cornish fisherman and legendary raconteur with son Danny, in St Ives Harbour. (*Courtesy of Yorkshire TV*)

In the fourteenth century Sloop Inn, St Ives, Dan Paynter in full flow. Willie Bish (with pipe) and Gascoigne Paynter, his audience.

Top: The ketch saved by a premonition – and the St Ives lifeboat.

Above: 'The picture that says it all' – the three children rescued from the ketch.

Left: Philip Moran – master mariner and the honorary secretary of the St Ives lifeboat.

The infant Tommy Cocking (far left) at the christening of 'The Caroline Parsons' in 1934.

Grace Darling – bending to the oars of her storm tossed boat.

The Tarts of Dungeness – lifeboat ladies who launched the hard way. (*Photo by Daily Mirror*)

A successful beach launch of the Dungeness boat.

Above left: Ron Cannon – coxswain of the Ramsgate lifeboat.

Above right: Cecil Roberts of Sennen Cove – one of the last Cornish wreckers. (*Courtesy of Mostafa Hammuri*)

Appledore – the bridge through which the chase happened.

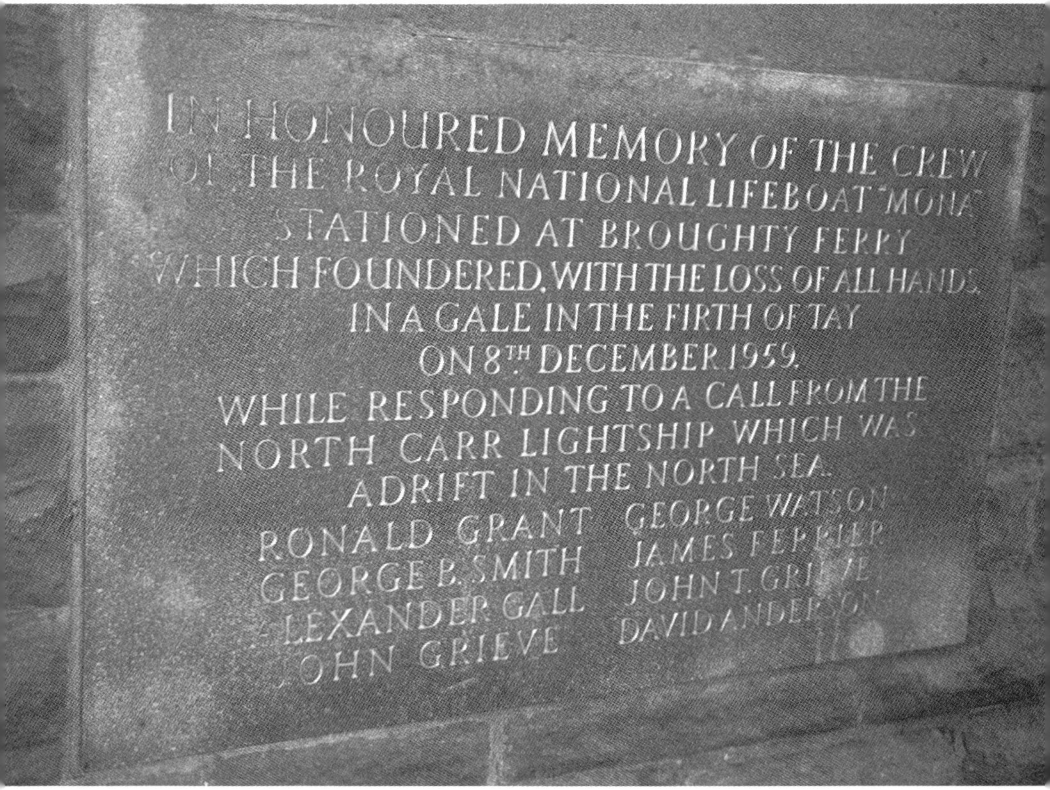

The memorial plaque for the men who perished in the Broughty Ferry lifeboat disaster.

The last of the sail/row lifeboats – Newquay, Cardiganshire, 1948.

tradition of service in the station that when de Courcy took over as honorary secretary in 1956, one son and two nephews of those lost were among the crew.

The doctor himself has not only a fascinating background, but once demonstrated a remarkable brand of courage himself – and at a ridiculously advanced age. He was born in India in 1911 to a Catholic mother and an Anglican father. His father was a brilliant linguist educated at Heidelberg University where he was appalled at the tradition of duelling with swords among students. He joined the Indian army and is believed to be the only Irishman to have died on active service in China during the First World War. He succumbed to typhoid. His son, who inherited his linguistic skill, went to Marlborough College, which he hated, desperately wanted to go to sea, and perversely joined a Dutch cargo ship as a steward at the age of seventeen. But after a couple of years he came ashore, won a history scholarship to Oxford University and launched into a distinguished career variously embracing journalism, forestry, harbour construction, university lecturing and maritime affairs which led to a double doctorate in law and philosophy.

But this true academic displayed a taste for action one night in 1978, when he defied both RNLI rules and time itself. A ship was reported in need of medical assistance close to the Kish Lighthouse in a force seven to eight gale. The telephone awoke Dr de Courcy at 2.30 in the morning. He was sixty-eight years old at the time.

'I got the crew and a doctor together and asked the cox to get in touch with the ship. It was first thought to be Greek, but turned out to be Iberian with a Spanish crew. None of them spoke English, and since I was the only one in our party able to speak Spanish it was clear I had to go.'

Dr de Courcy passes lightly over problems a pensioner must have faced trying to transfer from a small lifeboat to a large cargo vessel in conditions which threw both about in wild confusion. But he made it with much aplomb.

'The doctor and myself climbed aboard and were taken to this man lying on the deck. He looked so appalling that at first I thought he was dead. I asked the master what had happened, but all he was concerned about was making the next morning's tide at Greenock. He demanded that the doctor give the man an injection to keep him going. He was their second engineer, you see. I translated this to the doctor as he examined him, and he told me to inform the master that if the casualty wasn't taken ashore to hospital he would be dead long before any ship could get to Greenock.

'We had a slight argument!

'Then the rest of our crew came along and took him away and off to hospital where he was in intensive care for a long time before he began to recover. And from that day to this, we haven't heard from either the master or the owner of that ship. They weren't the slightest bit interested in the poor man. Talking to him, I found out that he was paid just sixty per cent of the salary a second engineer would receive on a British ship. In the end, I had to go and negotiate with the Spanish Embassy in Dublin to arrange his repatriation.

'I know I was breaking the rules when I went out on that service but I think that if you are in charge of a lifeboat crew you should be prepared to go with them. If I hadn't on that occasion, no one would have had any idea what was happening.'

23

The Marathon Men . . . and the Christmas Tragedy

Proceeding down the Republic of Ireland, past Wicklow, Wexford and Waterford, you arrive in the charismatic county of Cork, which has two lifeboat stations possessing a total of 300 years' continuous service between them: Ballycotton and Courtmacsherry Harbour.

But when it comes to sheer length of endurance, the men of Ballycotton must hold the all-time record for a particular marine marathon in February 1936. With coxswain Patrick Sliney at the helm, they set off to rescue the crew of the Daunt Rock Lightship, which had broken its moorings during the most powerful hurricane in local memory. So powerful that stones a ton in weight were torn from the Ballycotton quay and, in the words of the honorary secretary at the time, 'flung about like sugar lumps'. So awesome, in fact, that the cox decided not to fire maroons to avoid alarming the village, and those people who did see the lifeboat lurch anonymously out of the harbour went immediately to the church to pray.

Three days later the Ballycotton lifeboat returned home.

This historic mission has become one of the best known RNLI legends in a service crowded with tales of amazing feats. If you start a discussion about the RNLI service in the Republic of Ireland with any lifeboatman in Britain, the odds are that he will exclaim: 'Ah, yes – Ballycotton!' without any prompting.

Courage and patience do not often sit happily together, but Patrick

Sliney and his men displayed monumental reserves of both these virtues. For a long time the eight crew of the Daunt Rock vessel gallantly declined to abandon ship, keenly aware that a rogue lightship moving at the will of the elements instead of remaining in a fixed position could create fateful confusion amongst shipping. They were desperately trying to hold her steady with an anchor. A Royal Naval destroyer attempted twice to take her in tow – the lines being passed by the lifeboatmen – but each time they parted. Meanwhile, the storm raged on. The Ballycotton lifeboat was obliged to seek sheltered harbour twice to take on fuel, more rope, food and a change of clothing before returning to their epic battle. In the end, the crew of the lightship had to concede defeat as they were driven steadily towards the very rock after which their vessel was named. Five times Patrick Sliney manoeuvred under the stern and six men managed to jump aboard. The lifeboat's rails were smashed, the fender and deck damaged, and two men were still on the lightship, clinging to rails and seemingly unable to jump. Patrick sent men forward with orders to drag the paralysed pair off, at no little risk to themselves. As Patrick commented with grim humour afterwards: 'There was no time for "by your leave"!' The boat plunged forward a sixth time and in they came, injured in the process but not seriously. One of the rescued men later became hysterical, and had to be held down by two lifeboatmen to prevent someone being hurt or knocked overboard.

Patrick Sliney was presented with the gold medal, and his crewman son, William, received the bronze.

Thomas McLeod is the current coxswain of the Ballycotton boat and one of his crewmen is Colum Sliney, grandson of Patrick. Since taking over in 1977, Thomas has led over 300 missions, including one minor (by local comparison) marathon of his own. That occurred in 1979 when the Fastnet Yacht Race turned into a general fight for survival and the Ballycotton boat was out for almost seventeen hours in conditions described by the very modest Mr McLeod as 'really nasty . . . really dirty.'

Throughout their 138-year history, the Ballycotton lifeboat has come through all the hazards the sea can pose without losing a single crewman. Courtmacsherry Harbour, their sister station a little further down the coast of County Cork, cannot claim the same good fortune. In 1981 they lost one colleague in the most poignant of circumstances, trying to rescue him from his fishing boat.

There are many contrasting features between these two lifeboat communities. Ballycotton is a remote and, except for the yachting season, empty place, inhabited by reflective people who appear to be somewhat wary of strangers. Courtmacsherry, however, is an enormously convivial village and its lifeboat the hub of community life. Since there are no less then twenty-six qualified crew members, at least half the population seems to be committed in one way or another, and anyone arriving on lifeboat business is accorded a very warm reception. Everyone turns out, speeches of welcome are likely to be made by the cox, Diarmuid O'Mahoney, in the crowded pub (named, naturally, The Lifeboat) and hospitality offered in the splendid rambling old manor house called Barry's Hall owned by the honorary secretary, farmer and landowner Desmond G. Bateman. They all combine to make sure that guests will always remember Courtmacsherry and its lifeboat crew (which includes four women, as mentioned). This generous spirit apparently applies to all creatures. Once when the lifeboat was out, a pheasant shoot happened to be in progress in nearby woods. One bird escaped the pellets, headed off across the bay, but was too exhausted to make it and pitched into the sea. It was spotted by the crew, and a boarding boat was launched to retrieve it. Tenderly, it was brought ashore and placed back in the woods.

It is also a very musical place. The local band is famous for its own composition, The Courtmacsherry Lifeboat Suite, comprising five movements – the first symbolising a sailing vessel passing through the bay in fair weather, the second one depicting a storm approaching and placing the boat in peril, the third a lament for the loss of the boat, the fourth has the lifeboat starting up and launching, and the fifth is a jubilatory piece celebrating everybody being rescued! They played it at Truro Cathedral during a festival dedicated to the lifeboatmen of Cornwall and the Isles of Scilly. There is a strong social bond between Courtmacsherry and the southwest coast of England, cemented by regular exchange visits.

When a proposal to close down the station was mooted several years ago, the community rose as one to do battle. Their argument for its retention was eventually accepted, but they nearly lost it again at a later date when a move to Kinsale a few miles away was suggested. The harbour at Courtmacsherry was badly in need of dredging, and there had been an embarrassing moment when the lifeboat was launched on a call and got stuck.

Led by Desmond Bateman, who has served the lifeboat for more than thirty years, the locals flung themselves into remedying the situation, and, with a generous grant of £50,000 from the RNLI, saved the day once more.

After all, there had been a lifeboat in Courtmacsherry since 1825, and their illustrious history included going out to the *Lusitania*, the huge Cunard liner carrying almost 2,000 men, women and children, which was torpedoed twelve miles off the Irish coast in 1915 by a German submarine. Barely a quarter of those on board survived. Since 120 citizens of the United States were among the dead, including a Vanderbilt and several close friends of President Woodrow Wilson, the incident became a major factor in persuading America to go to war against Germany alongside the Allies.

The Courtmacsherry boat had the sad task of picking up many bodies. It was only in 1986 that the last survivor of that crew, Gerry Murphy, died aged over ninety, so the *Lusitania* is still well established in local folklore.

A much more recent painful memory concerned a Dutchman called Cornelius de Graff, who had lived and worked in Courtmacsherry and served with the lifeboat crew. He went back to his homeland to bring a thirty-two-foot steel fishing boat called the *Blue Whale* back to Ireland. On the way he called in at Newlyn, the major Cornish fishing port which neighbours Penlee lifeboat house.

As he prepared for the final leg to Ireland, the weather became ominous. The date was Saturday, 19 December 1981 and the elaborate Christmas lights were ablaze in Newlyn harbour. Cornelius de Graff had a companion aboard, but he wisely declined to continue sailing with him. So the Dutchman, who had a reputation as something of a daredevil, left alone . . . into the teeth of a hurricane.

The same night a coaster called *Union Star* reported engine failure eight miles east of Wolf Rock Lighthouse. The Penlee lifeboat, the *Solomon Brown*, was launched . . .

In Courtmacsherry that night the weather was as bad as anything they had experienced before when word came through to Desmond Bateman from men of the Cliff Rescue Service. They had spotted a boat near rocks west of the harbour.

'I alerted the cox and asked if it was possible to take the boat out. He said he could, but would probably have to stay out until the storm abated because of the difficulty in returning to harbour over the bar. As the lifeboat met its full fury, the glass windscreens bent alarmingly.

'It seems that Cornelius had been driven past the harbour, tried to find shelter between two rocks, Barry's Point and Horse Rock. At first we didn't know it was definitely him. But halfway through it all it was confirmed.

'I asked for a helicopter and an RAF Sea King was sent from Wales, but the weather played havoc with communications so they left after a vain search. The lifeboat could find nothing either, except a sleeping bag and bits of wreckage. No trace of Cornelius. Then it anchored in the bit of protection afforded by Barry's Point, but had to keep its engines running because of the conditions.'

Being trapped in the middle of a hurricane was not a pleasant situation to be in, but something happened which made it a thousand times worse. The radio was still tuned in as they tried to relax . . . and the news of the Penlee tragedy filtered through.

Eight men dead, every member of the crew. Their comrades in arms. Another eight on board the *Union Star* also perished, including two teenage girls. And somewhere much closer to home, one of their own . . . The emotional strain that must have caused can only be imagined, for those who experienced it tend to change the subject when it is mentioned.

They worked out what had happened to their crewmate when his boat was raised about a month later. Cornelius was still in the wheelhouse. The propeller and rudder were both bent to one side, obviously caused by an impact with a rock, which stopped the engine. It is supposed he went into the wheelhouse to see what was wrong and became trapped as the boat sank quickly.

Cornelius was wearing a life jacket, which meant had he been out on deck he would probably have been saved.

24

Valencia – and the Floating Battlefield

'Viking . . . Cromarty . . . Shannon, Rockall . . . Tiree, Stornoway . . . Scilly Automatic, Valencia . . .' The shipping forecast droning out from the radio has for decades been a family background litany to every household tuning in early to the six o'clock news. And many must have pondered idly, wondering just where those places were located, for some sounded distinctly foreign. German Byte, for instance. And Valencia? That has a definite Latin ring to it. Spanish, perhaps?

As a matter of fact, some would say it is easier to travel to Spain than to Valencia. It is an island off the west coast of the Irish Republic, approached via the Ring of Kerry, which fans out from Killarney through Macgillycuddy's Reeks and Moll's Gap close to where the Irish strawberry trees grow. The signposts on the way may be in miles, or in kilometres. They are not always specific. However, they often point in the right direction.

Truly, there is a gauntlet to run if you wish to visit Valencia, but a most glorious one, for the Ring of Kerry is possibly the most beautiful part of Ireland. The road may be perilously narrow and prone to writhing like a snake in pain, but there is an endless procession of superb seascapes to beguile the eye.

There is a sting in the tail of this journey. As Valencia finally hoves into view, there stands the main community of the island (and possibly the only one to justify that description, since the population barely totals 600), Knightstown, just a couple of hundred yards or so across the water. Almost close enough to conduct a conversation. The very place you want to be – but where is the bridge to take you across? Why, nine miles away at the other, basically empty end of the island. Eighteen miles later you arrive in Knightstown, puzzled.

'Sure, and most people seem to ask that question,' is the reply to well-restrained requests for an explanation about the position of that bridge. Like the signposts, the information is somewhat vague. All part of the charm of Ireland.

Valencia is just about the furthest flung outpost of the RNLI, and has stood guard over a wild stretch of the North Atlantic since 1864. Recently it has been distinguished for two reasons. First, it was obliged to deal with possibly the most unusual and unnerving mission any lifeboat has faced for many years. Secondly, the cox's first position on the lifeboat was: coxswain.

Seanie Murphy is a local man who went away as a youth to Lowestoft, where he spent five years on trawlers fishing out into the North Sea as far as the Orkneys and Shetlands. He became a highly qualified seaman and a possessor of a skipper's certificate. He arrived back in Valencia with his wife, a Kerry girl, just as the station was allocated the RNLI's top-of-the-range boat: an Arun, capable of a speed of eighteen knots. Seanie had fully intended to resume his fishing career locally but Paddy Gallagher, the honorary secretary, and the area inspector had other ideas. They needed a new cox, who had the proven skills to cope with the new boat.

'We both said Seanie's our man!' said Paddy.

That was in 1981, when Seanie was still only twenty-six – a mere stripling compared to the average cox. But he quickly justified their decision. On the second call out he was in the thick of it when a Spanish container ship broke up in Dingle Bay. Four years later in 1985 he launched on the most harrowing mission imaginable, the Air India disaster.

It was the morning of Sunday, 23 June, and Seanie was on his way to Mass.

'I met one of the lads working at the radio station and he said there may be a call for the lifeboat later that day because a jumbo jet had disappeared off the radar screen as it approached Shannon airport. I didn't think any more about it and went to Mass. When I came out I met Paddy Gallagher who had also heard that contact had been lost with the plane. Initially we were put on standby.'

According to Paddy Gallagher, there was a lot of confusion to begin with.

'I think the authorities could not believe what had happened, so they were slow to act. Then all hell broke loose.'

What had happened was a nightmare. A terrorist bomb had exploded on the plane, which was carrying 125 passengers, and the pilot didn't even have the opportunity to send out a Mayday. There were no survivors. It fell into the sea 120 miles off the coast, beyond the official range of the Valencia lifeboat. But Seanie Murphy didn't let that stop him.

'Because of the magnitude of the disaster we had no choice. I said we would keep going. When we reached the area there was no mistaking that it was the scene of an air crash. In fact, the lads said it resembled a battlefield. There were seats and debris and bits of luggage over a wide area – and the bodies. That affected us most. We picked up five, and one of them was a young girl. She couldn't have been more than nine or ten. It was the worst moment. One of our crew was only seventeen at the time and he was obviously very upset by that girl. He was never able to speak about it afterwards.

'The navy was down there with inflatables and divers, and RAF helicopters arrived. Some of the bodies were too badly mutilated for us to take aboard. If we located one like that we signalled for an inflatable to deal with it.

'I can see that scene now. It really is the one that sticks in my mind.

'On the way home we had to cut the engines back to conserve fuel. We had raced to get there and were fairly low on one of the engines. But we contacted a lighthouse twelve miles out to see if they could help. They gave us fifty gallons of diesel.'

Paddy Gallagher became the honorary secretary way back in 1967, and says that he had a baptism of fire.

'I'll never forget my first call out – 23 December 1967. It was a terrible night, storm force ten. Boats had been advised not to leave port, but the crew of one called the *Sea Flower* wanted to take their boat home to Castletown Bere for Christmas. They hit rocks at Ardgroom. What happened then was the saddest thing. There was an appalling lack of care on the part of some people. That boat was wrecked at quarter to nine at night. We were called out three hours later. In between those times they were hanging on with people on the shore just watching them, waiting to see what would happen.

No one thought to call the emergency services, and they couldn't call for help themselves because their radio was faulty. A member of the Garda eventually let us know. The lifeboat was only half an hour away from them when their light was seen to disappear. Five men, all drowned.'

In 1970, the cox of the Valencia lifeboat at the time, Dermot Walsh, won a silver medal in an exploit that had a bittersweet conclusion. A coaster called the *Oranmore* lay stricken off Kerry Head, and Dermot ran in five times to take off eleven men. Unfortunately, the *Oranmore*'s engineer, a very heavy man, plunged into the water from the breeches buoy as he was being hauled aboard the lifeboat and died of a heart attack.

Interestingly, the widow of the engineer sent the crew a massive bouquet and a letter expressing her gratitude to them for trying their best to save her husband. Of the ten who survived, not a thank you between them.

To balance the sad missions, the men of the Valencia crew have experienced the lighter side of lifeboating. An Archbishop who had been saying Mass at sea out in a small boat one Sunday evening went missing. When the midnight hour arrived with no sign of him there was an unholy uproar among all the emergency services – in complete contrast to the *Sea Flower* incident. The lifeboat found him floating safely in calm waters near Dingle Harbour.

On another occasion in 1979, a boatman dropped a party of about a dozen people, including a baby, on an uninhabited island. It did, however, have shelter. It was a Tuesday, and the boatman was supposed to collect them on the Thursday. But he forgot. The following Sunday a coaster reported by radio that people had been seen frantically waving flags and sheets from an island. The boatman arrived just as the lifeboat was taking them off. An interesting, if somewhat heated discussion took place!

Probably the most bizarre incident happened two years ago when a distress call was received from a boat which claimed to have run out of fuel twenty-five miles southwest of Valencia. When the lifeboat arrived alongside it they were rather taken aback to find a lone lady of seventy-eight years of age at the helm. And she had sailed all the way from Canada. It turned out she wasn't short of fuel at all – just lost. She was given five gallons of diesel anyway, and attempts were made to persuade her to allow the lifeboat to escort her safely to Valencia. But she refused, saying she was heading for Baltimore, a distance away on the tip of County Cork, where relatives were awaiting her. She was a small woman, and appeared to be frail, but she was very determined. So the lifeboat had to bid her a reluctant farewell.

She obviously became disorientated once again because she eventually came ashore at Goleen, more than thirty miles away from Baltimore. But she did send a cheque for 100 Canadian dollars to cover the costs of the lifeboat.

25

Reprimanded – for Saving a Life!

It could have been a scene from a feature film or a television series. Young girl, pretty, clad only in a bikini goes for a swim in the sea. Alone, innocent of an insidious tide which can turn and take a person into its icy grasp and carry her away to certain death. The girl feels its embrace, fights back, but the shoreline recedes further and further. The cold begins to numb her body and spirit. But she must hold on. The emergency services have been alerted. A helicopter is in the air, the lifeboat has been launched.

The girl is probably unaware of the bow of the lifeboat cutting at speed through the waves towards her. She begins to concede defeat, to slip away under the surf. A man hurls himself from the moving boat and reaches her side at the very moment she is about to disappear.

Happy ending. The girl is safe.

And what of the lifeboatman who performed this heroic act? A bronze medal, perhaps? Surely a commendation at least?

Derek Chambers, the cox of the Portrush lifeboat in Northern Ireland, smiles wryly when he is asked about the sequel to this stirring story.

'I was reprimanded by the RNLI Head Office for leaving the lifeboat!

'I wasn't the cox at the time, but I was the mechanic in charge of the engines. It was just a spur-of-the-moment thing. At first we couldn't find her, then the helicopter spotted her, told us on the radio and hovered over her to guide us in. She was just sinking as we reached her, so I jumped, and managed to grab her in time.'

An indication of how serious a condition the girl was in can be gauged by the time she had to spend in hospital – upwards of three weeks. Derek Chambers does not know whether or not she made a full recovery, because she hasn't been in touch, and several years have elapsed since the incident.

However, there is no bitterness in the man when you mention medals, and his response is swift and to the point: 'If you go out for medals, you shouldn't be in the lifeboat service.'

Nevertheless, there are people who consider that Derek Chambers should have been honoured – just for launching the Portrush boat on the afternoon of 13 February 1989.

No one is likely to dispute that on that particular day the lifeboatmen of Portrush faced the most horrific conditions in recent RNLI history. Maybe the worst ever. And there is dramatic photographic evidence for an enterprising local photographer took a series of stills which have been reproduced around the world. It is hardly possible to believe that any man, however brave, would venture out then. Those stunning pictures suggest that it was practically suicidal. Indeed, Derek Scott, the honorary secretary, and the man responsible for the management of the boat ashore, was desperately worried.

'It was off the Beaufort Scale. Twelve plus. Wind speed of 115 miles an hour. I live just opposite the boathouse and I was blown off my feet when I came out of the house. I had to cross the road on my hands and knees.'

The man in command of the boat, Derek Chambers, a quiet and reserved man, was nevertheless moved to describe the conditions as the worst he has ever experienced.

'Derek left the decision to me. I asked the crew, and they said, "Yes." There's not a lot to describe really. We had a good boat, but I suppose you had to know what you were doing that day. We didn't actually broach, but if I hadn't pulled the throttles back on one occasion she may have continued on a roll past the point of no return.'

There had been a report that two Spanish trawlers were in the grip of the hurricane and an immediate launch had been requested even before their exact position had been worked out. It later transpired that first one trawler had gone aground, then the other followed suit whilst attempting to assist. But they were in the shelter of Lough Swilly and not at serious risk at all. A local fishing boat pulled them both off at the next high water. But the Portrush lifeboat was already committed and in far more peril than the Spanish boats had ever been. A mixture of frustration and apprehension felt by Derek Chambers and his men must have been intense, but Derek shuns any opportunity to dramatise the event – the hallmark of courage. And two of his crew were on their very first service. No lifeboatmen can ever have had a more savage baptism.

'We were recalled after twenty minutes. But there was no way I could take the boat back into Portrush harbour. I had to run for shelter in Lough Foyle and that took three hours for what is normally less than a one-hour journey. Apart from the obvious problems, I also had to keep the crew's morale up. They were worried, naturally, so it was my job to put on a good show and bring them along with me.'

His skill finally brought the boat to calmer waters, but one man had to be taken to hospital with a cracked rib. The incident also gave birth to a legend, oft repeated when the Portrush men socialise in their favourite harbour bar. It concerns a moment at the height of the boat's battle with the storm when one of the youngsters out in the boat for the first time turned to a fellow crewman, who happened to be the accountant for the firm he worked for, and enquired anxiously whether he would be docked a day's wages because he was stuck in the lifeboat. The reply he received is regularly retold, to the poor lad's embarrassment: 'You stupid wee bitch – don't worry about a day's wages, worry about ever getting home!'

Someone enquired of the same youngster when he returned whether he had been seasick and he declared that he had not. He had been too scared to be sick.

Like many small harbours in Britain and Ireland, Portrush has virtually lost all its traditional fishing industry and now looks to tourists, sea anglers and yachtsmen for its financial survival. In times gone by the lifeboat was usually crewed exclusively by fishermen, but these days they are recruited from a wide cross section of the community. Derek Chambers, now turned fifty, is from the old school, a descendant of a Portrush family of long standing and the son and grandson of lifeboatmen. Now his crew include a builder, a college lecturer, a retired policeman, two school teachers, a plasterer, a civil servant and a local ballroom bouncer. Until recently they had a gentleman of the cloth in the crew and the honorary secretary, John Scott, had a good tale to tell about him.

'Brian Stuart, who has now moved to Belfast, was the curate for a time at the local Church of Ireland establishment. When he asked to join the crew, I said I would agree if he thought he could stand the colourful language which can sometimes be heard on a lifeboat! He became a well liked and much respected member of the crew, and he is particularly remembered for one occasion when he went out on the boat on a Saturday night on a service which turned out to be a very long job. I went round to tell his vicar that he would be late, and he was very concerned because the Bishop was due to visit that Sunday.

'Brian missed the Bishop. So the vicar detailed him to take evensong. But the boat didn't return until four in the afternoon and Brian was so tired that he fell asleep in the chair and missed evensong. The vicar was not at all pleased, so I pointed out to him that only one man had been able to walk on water and it wasn't Brian!'

Portrush suffered its share of the violence that put Ulster on the rack for so many years. Two policemen have been gunned down in its streets, buildings burned and some debris from a car bomb even landed in John Scott's back yard. But the divisions are not reflected in the crew, which has a refreshingly happy religious mix and a tendency to use humour to reduce any tensions.

This is well illustrated by another of John Scott's stories, concerning a recent trip across the water to Scotland to take the lifeboat into a shipyard for some maintenance and renewal work.

'It was a Saturday, so the crew went down to Glasgow for a night out. On the Sunday morning they felt a bit thirsty so one of the crew, who is a fan of Glasgow Rangers, led them to a Ranger's supporters club. They all had to sign in.

'The crewman who was a member told one Catholic colleague called Damien that he must temporarily rechristen himself George, and another must substitute Samuel for Christopher. He explained that Glasgow Rangers, being a Protestant club, might consider Christopher or Damien to be Catholic names, but they could choose William if they wished!

'The lads have had a lot of fun about that ever since. But we are used to working across a sectarian divide in Portrush. Our work often takes us to the Republic's coastline, and we can be in harness with a British helicopter one day and the

Irish Air Force the next. There's not time or inclination to worry about who follows what religion when the lifeboat is out there in a force nine gale trying to save some poor devil's life.'

26

The Menace of Ailsa Craig

The history of the Girvan lifeboat situated in the mouth of the Firth of Clyde is, to some extent, dominated by Ailsa Craig, a less than salubrious lump of rock which looms grimly out of the sea close to a port which was once a major source of herring, and a popular holiday resort for middle-class Glasgow, sixty miles away.

A mile and a half in circumference and 1,100 feet high, Ailsa Craig has historically been a magnet for unwary or stricken seaman. The roll call of ships that have come to grief there stretches at length down the years. About 700 years ago it was inhabited by monks who must have belonged to a particularly masochistic order. Since then, only people who have been obliged to earn a living have resided on Ailsa Craig. And lighthouse men, who are assumed to feel the need to seek a solitary life. No one is resident there now, but at one time around sixty men worked a quarry and they were regular clients of the Girvan lifeboat. In the days before sophisticated methods of communication, fires would be lit on designated parts of the island to indicate any problem. Once, around the turn of the century, one was spotted and the lifeboat crew were somewhat reluctant to go because of the prevailing conditions. But the signal meant that a quarry worker was injured so they launched. It took them seven hours to travel the nine miles to the rock, and they found the quarrymen had lit the fires as a protest because they were in dispute with their employers. There was no casualty.

The communication factor put the Girvan crew at some risk more recently when the Scottish skipper of a big Spanish fishing boat radioed in and announced he was dying. When the lifeboat arrived, she was starboard down, partly due to the violent weather and partly because all their fuel had unwisely been stored on that side, and the vessel was being taken by the prevailing wind towards Ailsa. A helicopter was hovering in the lee of the Craig, unable to approach the boat and take off the skipper because it was rolling so badly. It was imperative that the boat be steered downwind to achieve sufficient stability, but there was a problem. The skipper was too ill to do anything, and the rest of the crew were Spanish.

Cox Rod Leitch and his crew tried in vain to pass on this vital piece of information.

'It was like a scene from *Fawlty Towers*, with a lot of Manuels. There were fifteen Spaniards staring down at us, and sometimes up at us, saying, "*¿Qué, qué*?" Not one of them could understand a single word of English. The helicopter pilot even suggested going back to Prestwick to try and find an interpreter. All the time we knew we were getting closer to Ailsa Craig. It was so dark you couldn't see a thing – the lighthouse was on the other side. But you could smell it. So something had to be done and quickly. Since it was too dangerous to put our doctor on board, I asked our second cox, Stewart Moffat, and crewman John Warwick to risk jumping the gap. They made it safely. One grabbed the wheel and steered it downwind whilst the other prepared the sick skipper as the helicopter came in to take him off. He wasn't dying, but he was suffering from a stomach ulcer.'

Before he became cox when Colin McKechnie, who is now the honorary secretary, retired in 1991, Rod Leitch was involved in a drama which had a much smaller rock as its centrepiece. Called Craigskelly, it is a tidal rock situated only fifty yards offshore and accessible on foot – at low tide. Two Glasgow youths aged about fourteen, in Girvan on holiday in 1986 at a caravan site, walked out there with their fishing rods and stayed too long. They were cut off, and a force eight sprang up. They faced a long wait for the tide to turn, and it was feared they might panic and try to swim ashore.

As Colin McKechnie took the lifeboat as near as he dared, Rod and the second cox, Bill Patterson, went over the side with an X boat, an eight-foot inflatable dinghy with oars. They reached the rock, put life jackets on the youths and pushed them flat in the bottom of the dinghy. There was no room for Rod, so he hung on to the back and acted as a human drogue as it pitched and rolled through the surf to the beach where their mothers were waiting for them. Rod described the subsequent scene.

'It was quite wild. The police, the lifeboat and lots of other people were there trying to take down details as those mothers proceeded to give those boys a big whacking! I think they were in more danger ashore than on that rock. It turned into a double rescue, really, because the police had to step in.'

Perhaps the most fortunate man ever to be rescued by the Girvan boat was a former oil rig worker from Wales, who in 1986 bought a boat with the money he received when made redundant, and set off to go south from the Shetlands. He had had no previous sailing experience, which soon became painfully obvious to Colin McKechnie.

'He ran into bad weather. It seems that he had been advised in those circumstances to get all the sails down, go into the cabin and lock the door. Not try to anchor, just let it go. You could call it the ostrich theory. He followed that to a tee – except that he neglected to take down the sails. The boat had an engine, but he didn't bother to use it.

'He was spotted offshore in the surf about three miles away from Girvan. We had to use the X boat again, in very dodgy conditions, and managed to take him under tow. He was still below, waiting for things to happen.

'We took him ashore and dried him out. He thought he was in Barrow-in-Furness – which must be a couple of hundred miles south from here. Nothing could convince him that he was in the Clyde. Nothing. He spent three days here, and we got him some secondhand charts but he remained totally confused.

'He set off again, and we never heard another thing from him. I just hope his beginner's luck lasted out.'

When lifeboatmen pause to relate their more notable experiences, it is invariably – and understandably – the elders of the tribe who monopolise proceedings. The junior members, waiting in the wings for their chance, rarely get a shout. But one youngster in the Girvan crew already has had a taste of fame, albeit comic in every way. Richard Conagahan is still in his early twenties but already has more than four years' service to his credit and his keenness for lifeboating is very apparent.

His moment came during a local gala one very hot July Sunday when he was persuaded by his girlfriend to play a leading part in a float that she was organising. The theme was 'Alice in Wonderland'.

'They couldn't hire a cat suit but found a Garfield outfit, based on the cartoon character. So there I was, strapped up in a very large outfit which had to be packed out to fill the gaps because I am thin, being dragged through the town. It was very hot – the sun cracking the flags! I gave my pager to my girlfriend, who put it in her handbag. We ended up in a park where they held a competition for the best float, and we won. So everyone was celebrating when I heard this bleeping noise, and I thought someone was winding me up. But it was a genuine call. A yacht was in trouble. Now I was half a mile from the lifeboat, and I thought I had no chance of making it. But I started to run and when I got to the road I jumped out in the middle in front of the cars. I explained I was a lifeboatman on call, and one driver agreed to give me a lift. He was a bit wary at first. When he dropped me off I ran for the boat trying to get rid of the packing and peel off the outfit, watched by a crowd of tourists who were laughing and recording it all on their videos. I even made the local newspapers.'

27

The Son of the Island Crofter

No other lifeboatman can have travelled more extensively than Michael Currie, coxswain-mechanic of the Mallaig boat, situated on the west coast of the Scottish Highlands opposite Skye. He has circled the globe several times, and experienced many exotic lands and cultures – a veritable man of the world.

Yet he was fifteen before he saw his first railway train – or a frog, or a snake or even a deer. For he was born and raised in a place which had none of those things – Barra, the tiny island which nestles at the southern tip of the Outer Hebrides. Now in his forty-eighth year, Michael Currie can recall a childhood which had none of the comforts of life which the majority of people on the mainland have taken for granted for most of the twentieth century.

'I was twelve before electricity came to the island. Water was carried by pail from the well and every day after school I was sent up the hill to get a bag of peat for the fire. My father was a crofter and fisherman and he served in the merchant navy during the war. It may have been a simple life, but I think I had a better childhood than most city kids. We may have had no television, but among the older generation there was a tradition of storytelling, particularly by men who had been in the merchant navy. And you always had men coming in fresh from the sea. The first thing they did was to say hello to their parents, have a bath and a meal with a wee dram, and then off to visit their friends and neighbours with a bottle under their arm.

'Most of the men would congregate in the pub on a Saturday night, but there wasn't enough money around for them to go there every night so people would have house ceilidhs, impromptu music and conversation parties. If there was a dram available, then it would be offered. If not, cups of tea. But there was always lots of talk, sometimes until two or three in the morning.

'I would listen to the seamen and think that I would like to try that myself one day. At fifteen I crossed to the mainland for the first time in my life and went fishing from Mallaig for eighteen months. Then I applied to join the merchant navy.'

Michael Currie was approaching seventeen and the biggest place he had seen was Mallaig when he set off for London to become a merchant seaman. He claims the experience didn't bother him at all, but admits the inoculations against Third World diseases made him ill for three days. Within weeks, the innocent boy from Barra was in Kingston, Jamaica, with Australia the next stop. He loved it all.

'I went around the world four or five times. America, Canada, New Zealand, the Persian Gulf, the Suez Canal and round Cape Horn. Now I've never seen anything like the Horn at all in my life. It was calm – no wind at all – but a fifteen-metre swell sent water crashing down the deck towards the bridge.

'Four years later I was paid off in Germany and decided to go home. The first thing a boy from Barra did in those circumstances was to go to Glasgow and get a new suit from Burton's. So you would look respectable among the young lassies. At first I took a job with a contractor digging land ditches in the roads, the only land job I ever had. Then I went fishing again.'

Michael didn't join the Mallaig lifeboat crew until he was thirty-eight, but he was well known for providing back-up assistance with his fishing boat. Whenever he heard a Mayday on the radio he would slip his gear and often reach the vessel in distress before the lifeboat. Because of his experience and commitment, promotion came swiftly and he became cox in 1991. Recently he was able to save his own brother-in-law, who became stuck one morning whilst fishing in his twenty-eight-foot creel. He lay helplessly on a rock all day, and by the time the tide floated him off a force nine gale was blowing. His radar and his depth gauge had broken down, but mercifully, his radio remained operational so the lifeboat was alerted.

'By that time he was totally disorientated. Didn't know where he was or what course to take. When we arrived his boat was bouncing off the rocks, but he saw us and we were able to guide him out and escort him back to harbour.

'The most awesome situation I ever saw in the last few years happened when we went to the aid of a big, sixty-five-foot, steel clam dredger, which ran ashore in the narrows between Skye and the mainland, near the Kyle of Lochalsh. She was held broadside against the rock by the most amazing tide, unable to do anything. The lifeboat was recording a speed of seven and a half knots and standing still. We couldn't get near to the dredger and sent an inflatable to take off two men, not easy in that tide. Three stayed aboard to do what they could, and she came off in the end. But the pounding she took from that tide caused between sixty and one hundred thousand pounds' worth of damage.'

But Michael Currie nominates an experience he had on a fishing boat he once owned, the fifty-five-foot *Atlanta*, as the worst of his maritime career.

'That was the only time I have ever been frightened at sea. We were loaded up with sprats, thirty tons of them, and heading for Stornaway when we hit a westerly. I had a crew of five with me and since they had been working for a long time they had gone below. All were fast asleep. I was halfway around Ardnamurchan Point and about a mile offshore when the engine lost power – down to halfspeed. There was no real drive in the propeller so I assumed a plastic or Cellophane bag had wrapped around it. By then there was a full gale and a big swell and I had one hour and a half of praying, nursing it round. Thankfully I got her into a position where I could put her astern, and thrashed whatever it was off the propeller, something I couldn't dare do before when the boat was in a vulnerable position in case she fouled up altogether.

'The lads slept through it all. There was no point in waking them. I was, after all, the skipper so it was my sole responsibility.'

Further up the West Coast of Scotland, a comparatively young station has the responsibility of covering a massive area of seaway, all threatening by nature, and including the aptly named Cape Wrath.

Founded in 1967, Lochinvar now has an Arun-class lifeboat, the very best in the RNLI range, and its ability to work with speed and efficiency in conditions which would overwhelm most boats of its size has been tested on several occasions.

Neil Gudgeon, who has been cox for ten years, admits to 'some pretty nasty ones', including an aircraft coming down in the sea, although on a vastly reduced scale to the terrible disaster attended by the Valencia boat in Ireland.

'It was a private Lear Jet, with a senior French Air Force officer and a family of children on board, which crashed not far out from Stornaway. It was a very stormy night, with a force eight northeasterly which knocked out our radar, and it turned into a very large-scale operation with three lifeboats and a fishery protection vessel at sea, plus a Nimrod in the air. It went on for a period of three days and we found one body, a French Air Force officer. That was the first experience for most of the crew of actually pulling a corpse out of the water. And it had its effect. It took them some time to get over it, but it didn't put anyone off. They realised that someone has to do jobs like that.'

Much nearer home was the loss of a fishing boat from a neighbouring port. It put to sea two or three days after the New Year had been celebrated and ran into a storm.

'That was the last anyone saw of that boat or its crew. We searched all night and all the next night and found nothing. It was believed that the boat was pitching so violently that the engine went straight through the bottom. When something like that happens the whole community around here is affected.'

In common with other stations, Lochinvar has had its Spanish experience. In September 1994, a Spanish trawler had only just left Lochinvar harbour when it put out a call for help. Neil Gudgeon still laughs when he recollects what happened next.

'It was midnight and the weather dirty enough to prevent the helicopter from Stornaway landing here. The Spanish boat had run well aground and was starting to list when the tide went out. I manoeuvred alongside, and intended to take a few off at a time because the wind direction meant I couldn't lie close for too long without risking damage to the lifeboat. But the Spaniards panicked. They came swarming over the side, all eighteen of them at once, throwing their luggage and other belongings ahead of them! I had to stay close until the rush was over, or they would have all dropped into the water!'

28

Oil Rigs and a Roving Mechanic

In total contrast to the west coast of the Highlands, upon which nature has lavished the gift of sublime beauty, the east coast of Scotland lately surrendered its innocence on the altar of man's insatiable need for oil. Not that it ever had the same power to enrapture as its sister, but the eastern flank now has material compensations. Whereas the West echoes with a wistful emptiness as its children leave to seek a living elsewhere, the East has economic muscle and buzzes with activity.

Although most of the oil rigs are out of range of lifeboats, and generally have their own emergency services anyway, they can create a peripheral fallout which provides work on stations situated along the upper eastern coast of Scotland. A notable example is Invergordon, an RNLI station with a chequered history. It was first set up in 1911, closed in 1968, and reopened in 1974, as the oil industry changed the pattern of life in the Cromarty Firth.

Invergordon has never been more than a modest town, but it is rendered Lilliputian these days by the towering bric-a-brac of the rigs, at rest for one reason or another in the bay. Some have legs almost as thick as the Post Office Tower and are high enough to be on nodding terms with passing aircraft. Presumably great care must be taken in positioning them, for if one toppled over alongside the centre of Invergordon, it could lay waste half the town.

There is a highly unusual Sassenach flavour to the Invergordon branch of the RNLI. Although the cox, David Lipp, is from Aberdeen, their Waveney boat is called the *White Rose of Yorkshire* and the mechanic, Kevin Dent, is from the south of England. Since the mechanic is a key man on any lifeboat, very often full time, it indicates the cosmopolitan nature of the east coast. It is hard to imagine a similar appointment being made on a lifeboat in the Western Highlands.

Nor did this Sassenach have any seafaring experience before becoming involved with the Invergordon boat.

'I was born in the Basingstoke area of hampshire, and Hayling Island was the nearest I ever got to the sea. I came to Invergordon in 1980 simply because I loved Scotland, and eventually acquired a business doing shoe repairs and key cutting and selling fishing tackle and domestic electrical goods. About a year later the cox asked me if I was interested in joining the crew, which was a big honour for an incomer like me. Later on, the mechanic got a job on the oil rigs, and I succeeded him. I knew enough about engineering and mechanics to cope, and it seems I was the only person around who could leave work at any time to go on a call.'

The oils rigs can pose some unusual problems for lifeboatmen. None more so than the incident which stands out in the memory of Kevin Dent. It happened in December 1983, on one of the giant rigs stationed half a mile down the Cromarty Firth, and required action normally associated with a road accident.

'We got the shout at about five in the afternoon so it was dark when we arrived at this enormous thing. One of their rescue boats was being lowered with two men in it when something went wrong and it fell from a height of about 150 feet. The boat broke its back and one of the men became trapped in metal railings. They were wrapped around his body, and he was in a bad way. To make things worse the boat was sinking. His mate got away with a broken arm.

Two tugs on standby at the rig floodlit the scene as we pumped out the boat to keep it afloat and at the same time worked at cutting the man free with hacksaws. Meanwhile the doctor was trying to pump morphine into him. He was partly under water before we got him clear and into a basket stretcher with ropes underneath, so that we could lift him with as little movement as possible. He had broken his legs, arms, pelvis, and ribs. Fortunately he survived and he is walking again now. But that is the worst experience I have had to date on the lifeboat.'

Kevin Dent tells another story about a mission involving an oil rig which demonstrates once again that comedy often emerges to partly balance the pain and drama.

'It was another boat, this time bringing about eight men off a rig right at the end of Cromarty Firth. The night was foggy, the radar broke down and the boat went aground. We have a direction finder on the lifeboat and we were able to pinpoint him in a bay. But the tide was going out, so we got as close as we dared and sent a dinghy across to ferry the men to the main lifeboat. As that was happening the lifeboat also became stuck. The cox was pondering this problem when I noticed that the dinghy was full of water from men jumping in and out. So I volunteered to get in it and start baling. I was still in the boat when the cox began moving the lifeboat back and forth to try and free it from the sandbank. I shouted out, but it was too late. I fell into the water. But I was in no danger because I had got my life jacket on. So I was floating around and shouting for the crew to get a rope and rescue me. Then I felt something hard under one leg. I thought, That's funny, and tried the other one.

'I stood up and walked to the lifeboat! It was that shallow. That incident has become a standing joke with the crew – they never let me forget it.'

Further down the east coast heading south, there is another lifeboat mechanic who is both solidly Scottish, and possibly the most experienced of his kind in the entire lifeboat service. It is even more likely that no one has travelled further in the pursuit of his specialist duties.

Willy Pike is the full-time mechanic of the Broughty Ferry lifeboat, situated on the coast near Dundee. When Willy was seventeen, the man who rose to become the current Director of the RNLI, Lieutenant Commander Brian Miles, arrived in Ullapool in a seventy-foot lifeboat and offered him a job. That was twenty-eight years ago. For the next ten years he became a roving lifeboatman, moved not only around the coast of the British Isles, but all around the edge of Europe as well. Unsurprisingly, he can tell of a notable encounter with the Spanish.

'We used to go everywhere showing the flag – Portugal, France, Holland, Denmark, Germany, Sweden and Norway. We spent eight months in Spain on exercises and demonstrations and once went to the rescue of one of their trawlers which went on rocks in heavy seas near La Coruña, in the Bay of Biscay. Took a good few men off that one, we did.'

Willy's duties also took him to the far tip of his homeland at a time when tragedy struck twice within two years. He was in the Kirkwall boat which went out at the same time as that other ill-fated Orkneys lifeboat from Longhope, to the aid of a cargo boat aground on rocks off South Ronaldsay.

'I was probably the last person to speak to the Longhope men. I radioed them at twenty-five minutes past nine that night, 17 March 1969, just to ask them how they were getting on. They replied, "Not bad," and that was the last anyone heard of them. We were hitting seventy-foot waves that night. It was suggested we go through the Pentland Firth but we avoided that route, and probably saved our lives. The Longhope boat was found floating upside down by the Thurso crew who towed it into Scrabster, west of Thurso. We took the bodies back. Dan Kirkpatrick was the cox, and he had three silver medals which meant he had seen some action. We found him in the wheelhouse with his head rammed through the rails and his feet above the wheel. There was another crewman near him, but all the others were huddled together in the aftercabin. Eight men in total.

'I was also working the night the Fraserburgh boat capsized in 1970. Five of the six crew died, and the sole survivor happened to be someone I knew very well, Jackson Buchan.'

Eighteen years ago, Willy Pike married, and he was allowed to settle at Broughty Ferry, another Scottish station to be visited by disaster. In December 1959, their lifeboat launched to the aid of a light vessel reported to be adrift and didn't even make it over the notorious local sandbar. The present cox, Jim Hughan, knows it intimately.

'It has a very strong ebb, and in a southeasterly the sea rebounds off the sandbanks. The sea boils, and the marker buoys occasionally shift, which means you don't know where you are and cannot pick your spot. It must have been particularly fierce that night, and none of the eight lads survived.'

Jim Hughan and his crew believe they may have unwittingly come close to a sudden end themselves when a tanker laden with liquid gas went aground well up the Forth near Leith. They were launched along with the Dunbar lifeboat to stand by until a sister tanker could be brought to pump the gas out of the beleaguered boat.

'It was blowing a hooley, and we were out there for three days, alternating with the Dunbar boat. What nobody told us at the time was that if the tanker's refrigeration broke down the gas would expand and go walkabout. Apparently, it would then hang around in a big ball until it either dispersed – or found something to ignite it.

'Neither did they inform us that, as we were pitching around out there by the tanker, the army had been called in to be ready to organise the evacuation of the entire town of Leith!

'When it all finished we went across to Dunbar to have a chat about it with their lads. By that time the boat had been refloated and was anchored downwind. We were sitting around having a chat and a cigarette when they started to vent the tanks. When the smell hit us we realised that one cigarette lit at the wrong time could have blown us all up!'

29

Hell's Mouth . . . and the Return of the Devil!

This journey around a random selection of communities where the call of the running tide must be answered began in St Ives, Cornwall, and will end there. Conclude, indeed, in the company of a man who is a classic example of this special breed, one who has faced up to the sea in all its guises, benevolent and malevolent, and won through to tell the tale by dint of courage, wit and a dash of sheer good fortune.

And when it comes to telling a tale, Dan Paynter has few equals. Like Coleridge's Ancient Mariner he can hold an audience spellbound when the mood takes him. His reputation has spread far beyond Cornwall, for he was the central figure of a major television documentary in the 1970s, had a significant role in another based on the St Ives lifeboat, and the unfailing ability to conjure up a quotable line, delivered with a rich Cornish flavour, has made him a perennial target for reporters from all branches of the communications industry.

The Paynters have probably been the most influential family in St Ives harbour for generations, and traditionally the biggest employer of labour. Paynter boats have taken fish from the sea in winter, and visitors on trips around the coast in summer in numbers far beyond computation. A voyage to Seal Island has been the first glimpse of wild life for maybe half a million or more holidaymakers as the Paynters capitalised on the appeal of a colony of grey Atlantic seals on a rock a couple of miles along the peninsula towards Land's End. A typical example of Dan Paynter's ready wit was once heard when a lady returned from a Paynter trip and stood at the bar of the Sloop Inn complaining that no seals were to be seen.

'Ah, well, m'dear, you see this time of year we 'as 'em in for painting!'

The fourteenth-century Sloop Inn is already listed as a building of historical importance but Dan's customary corner in the Fisherman's Bar should, perhaps, be placed in a special category of its own. For at least forty years, people from all around the world have gathered there, fascinated by the music of Dan's tales of a thousand and one experiences at sea. He served in the Royal Navy during the last war, and was in the middle of the mayhem of Utah beach during the Normandy landings, and has been decorated for bravery whilst serving in the St Ives lifeboat. From boyhood he has pursued fish from the English Channel to the Republic of Ireland. He has a rare ability to locate profitable shoals, and a vast knowledge of the ways and vagaries of the sea.

His RNLI medal was awarded for his part in an extremely unusual mission – the rescue of a group of potholers. They had descended by rope down into a cave which has two entrances to the sea at a place just round the corner from St Ives Bay called, appropriately, Hell's Mouth. When the time came for them to leave as the tide rose, the rope had become slippery with dripping water. One man sustained serious head injuries as he fell in attempting to climb out, another managed to swim out and raise the alarm.

It was 9 August 1958, and St Ives carnival was in full swing when the maroons exploded in a cloudless sky. It was a glorious day, and Dan Paynter, busily ferrying people to and from Seal Island, had just moored up for another boat load.

'It was flat calm and we thought there would be nothing to it. We towed one of my skiffs behind the lifeboat and took it into the cave, me, my cousin Jack Paynter, Martin Roach and Tommy Cocking. I was just saying to the others that it wouldn't take long to sort this all out when in came a range. That's a rising ground sea which always comes in threes. Fierce it was, and making a terrible noise. We couldn't hold on to the boat and away it went. Smashed to pieces, it was. So there we all were, trapped as well. One of us had to get out, to tell the others on the lifeboat, and I said I would go. I cannot swim, but I had my life jacket. So

I tucked one of the young potholers, a girl of about fourteen, under my arm to take her with me but she screamed so much that I had to bring her back. I was knocked back two or three times but eventually I emerged. When Mike Peters, the engineer, saw me he jumped overboard and got me back on the lifeboat where I told Dan Roach, the cox, what the position was. We collected together every bit of line on that boat, rocket lines as well, and every available life jacket. Mike went into that cave on his own pulling everything behind him – Dan Roach wouldn't let me go back because he said I had done enough. They had a spot of bother with the injured potholer, who was Swedish. He said he would rather not go, but Jack Paynter had a word with him! They put life jackets on, got lashed on to the lines and we pulled them out, all seven of 'em. Popped out like a row of corks, they did.

'I had the day's takings in my pocket through all this and Father had to hang it out to dry!'

The exploit merited a clutch of medals and wide news coverage. Mike Peters was awarded the silver, Dan Roach and Dan Paynter a bronze each, and the rest received certificates. A local potter produced a range of commemorative mugs bearing all the names of those involved, and the RNLI organised a medal presentation ceremony in London.

This apparently proved something of an ordeal for a certain member of the Royal family. A problem of communication arose, based on the Cornish pronunciation of certain words, when the Royal personage came face to face with this rumbustious group of seafarers hellbent on having a good time in the capital city. Dan Paynter remembers the occasion very clearly.

'We had to go and see the Duchess of Gloucester, poor old soul. A very small lady she was, and quite frail. We were all down below in Westminster Hall drinking tea when one of the Institution's men came to me and said the Duchess wished to meet me and hand over the medal. I asked him what I should say to her, and he advised me to ask about her children. It seems they had measles. Anyway, I went into this room and there she was. We shook hands, and she was trembling and shaking like a blind boy taking snuff! And to tell the truth, I was the same.

'I said to her, "How's the childer?" And she said, "I beg your pardon?" So I asked her again. But she still didn't understand.

'What a night we had. There were other lifeboatmen down to

receive medals, including the cox from Lerwick in the Shetlands, and we were all given a sum of money to have a good time. Supposed to last the night it was, but we weren't going more than an hour before it all ran out. We ended up paying for the damn night out ourselves! They put us up in a hotel opposite Buckingham Palace, but there was no sleep to be had. Dan Roach woke me up at four o'clock in the morning to complain that he had been kept awake all night by horses going up and down the road. They must have been changing the guard.'

A few years previously, Dan had found himself under guard when the Irish Navy arrested his boat for poaching. They were fishing for herring – just six miles off the Republic's coast.

'We had only hauled 6 cran – that's about 112 stone – when I saw 'em. They put a searchlight on us and rowed across in a whaler with fixed bayonets, wearing crimson tassels on their hats like the German Navy. The war wasn't long over and nearly all our crew had been in the navy, and when Jack Wedge watched them approach us, he said: "Look, the bloody Germans are here again!"

'We were taken into close arrest under armed guard to Dunmore, and the skipper, John Madden Veal, was put in prison for three days. They patrolled the harbour all night. Our nets were confiscated, and they thought they had all our catch, too, but we hid a lot away down below in dustbins. The Irish press came aboard to interview us, and we sang Cornish songs for them.

'John was brought into court at Waterford and fined £100, a lot of money in those days. But Paddy O'Toole, the man who used to buy our fish, not only paid the fine but bought our nets and presented them back to us. We all got on very well with the Irish. We used to steam two hours up to Waterford and always carried a basket of fish for the children. Real poverty there was in Ireland in those days – mothers carrying children, begging in the street for pennies. We used to give 'em the basket to help themselves.'

On 5 March 1962, St Ives came close to losing its high-profile son during an incident which had the entire town in a state of nervous anxiety for an entire day. It became one of the most popular stories in the remarkable repertoire of Dan Paynter.

'Lovely day to start with, it was. Seven of us set out to go fishing in the *Lamorna*, a brand-new forty-seven-foot boat, and headed about fifty miles offshore, passing other boats on the way. The Cornish fleet was all out, Newlyn men as well. We shot our long lines and after three or four hours we had a nice bit of fish. Just as we were finishing hauling, the skipper, Willie "Bish" Care, exclaimed: "Look, all the other boats are going westward."

'We wondered why this was, since most of the fish were in the other direction. Anyway, we had twenty baskets of bait left so off we went on our own like heroes to the east. The weather was still as good as it could be.

'Before the sun went down we knew why those boats went westwards. They were going home. A force ten gale had been given out on the radio and they heard it. But we had no radio! All we had on that boat was a compass. The wind freshened from the southeast and then it started. That night we saw seven lighthouses – not the lights directly but the looming in the sky, which means only one thing. Bad weather. In fact it got so rough we couldn't even go out on deck. It was underwater. There were three of us in the wheelhouse pulling in our lines over the sternboard until we had all our gear. I recall the last fish we had – it was a turbot.

'Then we went below to take spells at pumping. We had to keep the engines out of the water at all costs. Fourteen hours we were pumping. We couldn't steer because the sea was in control. The log told us we had travelled a quarter of a mile during one two-hour period. Then a wave hit us and the boat was thrown about – just like a piece of wood coming in on the beach. We were going side afore. And a lot of the gear went over the side.'

Whilst the marathon fight for survival was going on, the *Lamorna* was posted as missing, and distressed relatives and friends gathered in St Ives harbour convinced they would never see Dan and his shipmates again. There was no point in sending out the lifeboat because no one had any idea where they were. A plane searched in vain, although it was heard overhead on two occasions by the crew of the *Lamorna*.

Late in the afternoon of the next day, a boat was spotted by watchers on the quay. Through the spray still being kicked up by the storm it was joyfully identified as the *Lamorna*, and crowds piled into the harbour as word spread around the community. The sight of home came as a surprise to the crew of the *Lamorna* as well, as Dan recalls.

'We were only 200 yards away when we realised we were just

outside St Ives harbour, but it was still too bad to put in there. The punt we left at the moorings had been sunk. There were twenty-two ocean-going ships sheltering from the storm in St Ives Bay at the time. So we went very carefully up the river to Hayle, and when we tied up half the town was there to greet us. A pal of mine, Henry Symons, handed over a bottle of rum and told us to go below and drink it. We did!

'Now we had to stay with the boat because the fish needed gutting, and we also required a leg to keep the boat upright. So Willie Bish sent his younger brother, John, one of the crew, over to St Ives to fetch one. He is married to a Catholic girl. He was gone for four or five hours. When he came back Willie Bish demanded to know where the hell he had been.

'"Strange thing, Willie," he said. "When I got home the house was in darkness. I popped my head into the front room and I saw seven candles burning, and Father Delaney praying. He had lit a candle for each member of the crew."

'Willie then asked John what they had said when they saw him.

'"Well," said John, "Father Delaney looked up and, said: "'Blow them out. The devil has returned!'"'

Index

Note: illustrations are indicated by *il.*